CLOUDS

First published in April 2019

British Library Cataloguing in Publication Data
A catalogue record for this book is available
from the British Library.

ISBN 978 1 78521 636 7

Library of Congress catalog card no. 2019930122

Published by Haynes Publishing,
Sparkford, Yeovil, Somerset BA22 7JJ, UK
Tel: 01963 440635
Int. tel: +44 1963 440635
Website: www.haynes.com

Haynes North America Inc.
859 Lawrence Drive, Newbury Park,
California 91320, USA

Designed by James Robertson
Cover by Mecob

Printed and bound in Malaysia

CLOUDS

ALL YOU NEED TO KNOW IN ONE CONCISE MANUAL

Storm Dunlop

Contents

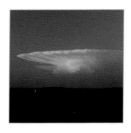

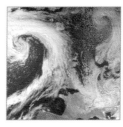

Introduction

Frequently in the past and still nowadays, many people find clouds confusing. The problem is that they seem to change continuously. For many centuries, it seemed utterly impossible that anyone could devise any way of describing them accurately. The major features of animals and plants did not change, so with them it was possible to describe what they were like and compare one with another. But when it came to clouds, they were always moving and changing. One minute you might look at them but the next they had drifted off and altered in shape.

Many early paintings showed clouds that were utterly unlike real clouds. They were often stylised and merely included as decorative elements or else because they were given some symbolic value. Only with the growth of interest in landscape painting did artists start to pay more attention to the form of clouds. Otherwise, clouds were largely neglected by those interested in general scientific studies, even those relating to meteorology.

→ A detail from the 15th century fresco *The Legend of the True Cross* by Piero della Francesca showing symbolic clouds. *(Getty Images)*

*"Can any man read
the secret of the
sailing clouds...?"*

JOB, 36, 29

Chapter 1
Discovering clouds

Clouds are nearly always present in the sky, yet to most people their types and names remain mysterious. Similarly, many people have little idea of how clouds can help to forecast coming weather. At times, ever-changing, clouds may seem to offer little hope of making any sense. Our understanding of the nature and types of clouds changed thanks to just one man – Luke Howard.

← Cumulonimbus clouds gathering over the sea. *(Shutterstock)*

'The Father of Meteorology'

At long last, one enthusiastic weather-watcher had seen so many clouds that he realised that there were similarities and differences that could be described. That person was Luke Howard – *see box opposite.*

Howard had realised that there were certain basic forms of cloud that were recognisable, even though the exact shapes might differ. Just as Linnaeus had used Latin names to describe plants (in 1753) and animals (in 1758), so Howard used Latin terms to describe the basic types of cloud. Although the scheme has been greatly modified and expanded in the years since 1803, some of Howard's terms are still in use. These include 'cirrus' (Latin: *a curl or lock of hair*); 'cumulus' (Latin: *a heap*); 'stratus' (Latin: *a layer*); and 'nimbus' (Latin: *a halo* and, by extension, *rain*).

Howard's scheme showed how the form of clouds was related to the way in which they had been created. Its merits became widely recognised by authors, poets and painters, as well as by the scientific community. His work was the inspiration for Percy Bysse Shelley's poem *The Cloud* (see page 32).

Howard corresponded with Johann Wolfgang von Goethe, the great German

← A watercolour by Luke Howard, of cloud now known as cumulonimbus.
(Getty Images)

↓ A watercolour by Luke Howard, entitled *'Light Cirro Cumulus above Dorset'*.
(Getty Images)

writer and statesman, who had a significant interest in scientific subjects. Goethe was greatly impressed by Howard's cloud classification scheme and even included thanks to him in a series of poems.

Howard's work was also taken up by various painters, such as Richard Bonington, and most notably by John Constable, who made a series of paintings of clouds, annotated with full details of the weather conditions at the time and using Howard's classifications. These are so detailed that present-day meteorologists are able to reconstruct the weather on the days involved. Constable was particularly interested in showing clouds correctly, considering that it was essential in his landscape paintings. He called his cloud studies 'skying'.

"But Howard gives us with his clear mind
The gain of lessons new to all mankind;
That which no hand can reach, no hand can clasp
He first has gained, first held with mental grasp."

Johann Wolfgang von Goethe, *writer and statesman*

Luke Howard

Luke Howard (1772–1864) has come to be known as 'The Father of Meteorology'. He was born in London and became a pharmacist. He later established himself as a manufacturing chemist. Although initially mainly interested in botany, he soon became obsessed with observing clouds. He realised that it was possible to recognise specific forms and that these could be classified. Although not the first to suggest such a cloud classification scheme, he put forward his own classification in an essay, *On the Modifications of Clouds*, presented to the Askesian Society in 1802, and published in 1803. He proposed a formal classification of clouds, similar to that used by Carl Linnaeus for plants and animals. His proposals were widely accepted and some of his terms remain in use today. The classification scheme was successful because he recognised (and allowed for) changes in the form and structure of clouds.

(Getty Images)

LUKE HOWARD 1772–1864 Namer of Clouds lived and died here

← Realistic clouds in the painting *Wivenhoe Park* (1816) by John Constable. *(Wikipedia)*

Charles Piazzi Smyth

(Wikipedia)

Charles Piazzi Smyth, FRS (1819–1900) was involved in astronomy, meteorology and Egyptology. He was Astronomer Royal for Scotland from 1846 to 1888. Like many Victorians, he drew and painted many subjects on many different occasions, and these included paintings of clouds (see page 13).

He was the first to photograph clouds in detail, initially with the aim of showing how they changed and developed. To do this, he devised a special camera and accumulated more than 500 cloud images. A selection of these were published in three large volumes in 1897. Unfortunately, he included clouds because he considered them as objects of beauty and manifestations of the bounty of God, so these photographs, despite being accompanied by plentiful observational data, were largely ignored by the scientific establishment when it came to the compilation of the *International Cloud Atlas*, which remains, to this day, the primary reference source for information about all the varied forms that clouds may take.

Piazzi Smith visited Madeira in 1881 to investigate its suitability for an astronomical observatory, and published a book *Madeira Meteorologic* (1882), in which he described and illustrated a 'remarkable cloud' that we now recognise as altocumulus lenticularis (see page 69).

In later life, Piazzi Smyth became preoccupied with Egyptology and developed extravagant theories about the significance of the Great Pyramid at Giza. He resigned from the Royal Society when they would not wholeheartedly accept his ideas. He carried his mania to the grave: His tomb is shaped like a pyramid.

➔ *Salisbury Cathedral from the Bishop's Garden* (c. 1825) by John Constable. *(Wikipedia)*

Howard's scheme came well before photographic techniques were discovered and the first attempt to photograph clouds was made, much later, by Charles Piazzi Smyth in the 1870s. Previously, Piazzi Smyth had made many paintings and drawings of clouds. Eventually, in 1897, he published three volumes of cloud photographs.

⬇ A painting of altocumulus clouds by Charles Piazzi Smyth.

Further studies of clouds

Others took up the study of clouds through photography. Arthur Clayden published his book *Cloud Studies* in 1905. He, like Piazzi Smyth, was particularly interested in the beauty of clouds and the way is which they were poorly represented in art.

↑ George Aubourne Clarke.

The International Meteorological Committee published the first standardised list of names for cloud types in 1896 in the first edition of the *International Cloud Atlas*, and also proposed an international year of cloud photography to take place in 1897–8.

One notable photographer was George Aubourne Clarke (1879–1949) of Aberdeen. He was the observer at Aberdeen University's Cromwell Tower Observatory between 1903 and 1943.The first edition of his book of cloud photographs, *Clouds; a Descriptive Illustrated Guide-book to the Observation and Classification of Clouds*, was published in 1920 and went on to become the standard reference work on cloud forms.

"To the artist I trust they may also be of some use, by calling attention to the variety and exquisite beauty of the sky. Nothing is more extraordinary in art than the general negligence of cloud-forms. Many of them are quite as worthy of careful drawing as the leaves on a tree ... Yet it is the common rule to find pictures, which are otherwise marvellous examples of skill and care, disfigured by impossible skies with vague, shapeless clouds, as untrue to nature as it would be possible to make them."

Arthur Clayden, *Cloud Studies*, 1905.

Appreciating clouds

Clouds still continue to exert their fascination on everyone, as indicated by the recent formation and rapid growth of the Cloud Appreciation Society. They do, however, occasionally have unexpected consequences.

This was the case with James Glaisher, the nineteenth-century meteorologist and pioneering balloonist. He began his working life as a surveyor in County Galway in Ireland. He later said that his surveys were so often frustrated by clouds that he became, of necessity, interested in meteorology.

James Glaisher

James Glaisher (1809–1903) was born in London. After his initial work as a surveyor and a spell of astronomical work at Cambridge, he became assistant to the Astronomer Royal, G.B. Airy, at Greenwich, and eventually became Superintendent of the Magnetic and Meteorological department at Greenwich.

He became famous for his ascents in balloons to obtain meteorological observations, in particular an ascent in September 1862, when with Henry Coxwell, the balloonist, the balloon reached a height of about 29,000ft (approximately 8,840m, or roughly the height of Mount Everest), where he became unconscious through lack of oxygen. The balloon continued to ascend to a height later estimated to be well above 30,000ft – some estimates put the altitude as high as 37,000ft (11,280m) – at which Coxwell, who was unable to use his hands, struggled into the balloon's rigging and managed to pull the gas-release cord with his teeth, causing the balloon to descend.

(Wikipedia)

(Getty Images)

GREATER LONDON COUNCIL

JAMES
GLAISHER
1809–1903
Astronomer, Meteorologist
and pioneer of
weather forecasting
lived here

Inspiring clouds

In 1894, Charles Thomas Rees Wilson spent a short period as relief observer at the Ben Nevis Observatory that was then situated on the mountain.

He found that the appearance of coronae (coloured rings seen around the Sun – see page 102) and a glory (a set of coloured rings that appear around the shadow of an observer's head – see page 104) were particularly striking.

These inspired his later work for which he received the Nobel Prize for Physics in 1927. His experience of being surrounded by a thunderstorm on Ben Nevis in 1895 also led to his interest in electrical phenomena.

"In September 1894, I spent a few weeks in the Observatory which then existed on the summit of Ben Nevis, the highest of the Scottish Hills. The wonderful optical phenomena shown when the sun shone on the clouds surrounding the hill-top, and especially the coloured rings surrounding the sun (coronas) or surrounding the shadow cast by the hill-top observer on mist and clouds (glories), greatly excited my interest and made me wish to imitate them in the laboratory."

C.T.R. Wilson, *Nobel Lectures*, 1947

Charles Wilson

Charles Thomson Rees Wilson, FRS (1869–1959) was a distinguished physicist and Nobel Prize winner. Born at Glancorse in Midlothian, he studied at Manchester University, then moved to Sidney Sussex College, Cambridge, where he gained first-class honours. Initially a teacher, he returned to the Cavendish Laboratory in Cambridge in 1894. There, following his experience at Ben Nevis, he carried out experiments into how condensation occurred in clouds. He discovered that condensation could occur when charged particles passed through his experimental chamber. Also at the Cavendish Laboratory was J.J. Thomson, who carried out the experiments that demonstrated the existence of the particle known as the electron, for which he was awarded the Nobel Prize in 1906. He used Wilson's cloud chamber to determine the charge on the electron.

Wilson studied atmospheric electricity for a while, but returned to his cloud-chamber work in 1910, and eventually, after various refinements, found that he could determine the track of a single charged particle through the chamber. This proved to be a vital tool in the investigation of atomic physics and the reason Wilson received the Nobel Prize in 1927.

Cloud-watching today

Although Luke Howard recognised certain sub-types of cloud, later observations have enabled meteorologists to describe a host of species and varieties that have distinct characteristics (see Chapter 3) and even some new major types (genera).

Research has also revealed how clouds develop and evolve, and the principal methods by which they form are described in Chapter 2).

Clouds are also relevant to the study of forthcoming weather. In particular, modern satellite images of the clouds associated with tropical cyclones (also known as hurricanes and typhoons) and the depressions (more properly known as extratropical cyclones) provide useful clues as to how a storm is likely to develop and how destructive it may be. Superstorm Sandy, which devastated New York and New Jersey in 2012, is an example. The extremely large cloud cover gave an indication of how large the storm had become and how great an area would be affected.

And then there's global warming and climate change. It might appear that clouds are a minor factor to scientists – working with supercomputers and atmospheric models – who are trying to understand how the weather and climate will change in the future, but actually, clouds are extremely important. Some

⬆ Two satellite images of tropical cyclone Benilde in the southern Indian Ocean, taken on 30th and 31st December 2011. *(NASA)*

species and varieties of clouds act to reflect sunlight back into space, thus cooling the Earth, whereas others prevent heat from the atmosphere and surface escaping to space, causing greater heating. Understanding the effects of clouds is one of the major difficulties in predicting how conditions will change.

Although weather forecasting and climate change are not discussed in this book, clouds remain of fundamental importance to both, so the descriptions given in the following chapters are actually relevant to all aspects of meteorology and climatology.

The finest and sweetest water
is every day carried up
and is dissolved into vapour
and rises to the upper region,
where it is condensed again
by the cold and so returns to
the earth.

Aristotle, *Meteorologia*, 350 BC

Chapter 2
The formation of clouds

Clouds consist of water droplets or ice crystals, and so to understand how clouds form, evolve, and die away, it is helpful to know a little about the properties of water (and ice), and also how air temperatures change in the atmosphere. It is also helpful to learn a little about topics such as humidity and stability, which may sound rather technical, but are actually quite easy to understand.

← Spectacular cumulonimbus clouds, threatening heavy rain.
(Shutterstock)

Water

Water is an interesting substance, with unusual properties. Water occurs in three different forms (known as phases): as a solid (ice); liquid and vapour.

People tend to think of water vapour in terms of steam (condensed water droplets), but water vapour is actually an invisible gas, comprising individual water molecules. When a kettle boils vigorously, the 'gap' between the spout and the visible steam is actually the invisible water vapour. Such invisible water vapour is present everywhere in the atmosphere – even though it may be in minute amounts, for example over deserts. Only when it condenses into droplets (such as cloud or fog droplets) does it become visible.

Humidity

The air always consists of a mixture of gases, including oxygen, nitrogen, and water vapour. Humidity is a measure of the amount of water vapour in the air. In general, the higher the temperature, the more water vapour is in the air, and so the greater the humidity. As air cools, perhaps due to rising in the atmosphere, the amount of water vapour that it is able to absorb decreases. Eventually, the temperature drops to what is known as the dewpoint, when the water vapour condenses into tiny droplets of liquid. If the parcel of air is freely floating, this causes a cloud to form. If the dewpoint is reached at ground level, the water is deposited as dewdrops.

Condensation nuclei

The condensation of water vapour into liquid droplets is not completely straightforward. For a water droplet to form, it requires a tiny solid particle as a 'condensation nucleus'.

Typical nuclei are dust particles, crystals of salt (from sea spray), certain chemicals (some of which are produced, directly or indirectly, by algal blooms in the oceans), bacteria, and even the tiny outer plates shed by certain bacteria. These particles are so plentiful everywhere on Earth, that water droplets may form anywhere, even over the driest deserts. Cloud droplets are typically about 100 times the size of a condensation nucleus.

The formation of ice crystals

A solid nucleus is also required for ice crystals to form, but this must be of a specific shape for the water molecules to freeze into place. Although the sources of such particles are as varied as those of condensation nuclei, because they need to be a particular shape they are not nearly as plentiful and they are often absent from large regions of the atmosphere.

In the absence of a suitable nucleus, a water droplet may exist at temperatures far lower than 0°C, in what is known as a supercooled state. This often occurs in the atmosphere, and such cold droplets freeze instantaneously when they come in contact with either a suitable particle or a solid surface. This often happens when aircraft fly through regions where there are plentiful supercooled droplets, particularly in middle-level clouds, such as altostratus (see page 45).

On rare occasions, supercooled raindrops reach the ground and come in contact with roads and other objects that

The ice storm of 1998

One of the most notable ice storms affected a wide region of eastern Canada and the north-eastern states of the USA in 1998, causing major disruption of electrical supplies and transport, several deaths, and the loss of large numbers of livestock.

Three pulses of warm, moist air from the Gulf of Mexico moved northwards and encountered a frigid air mass from Arctic Canada. Here, the warm air rose above the cold, and produced plentiful rain. The raindrops fell into the layer of air closest to the surface, which was well below freezing. The raindrops became supercooled as they fell, and froze instantly when they hit the ground or objects such as trees, telephone and electricity lines, poles and pylons, which were weighed down by the weight of ice and either collapsed or broke.

⬆ One of the many electricity pylons, damaged in the 1998 ice storm. *(Getty Images)*
⬇ The rain froze instantly when it hit cold objects such as these cars. *(Getty Images)*

are well below freezing. They then freeze immediately into a clear layer of ice (known as 'glaze' or sometimes called 'black ice'). Such conditions are the cause of occasional 'ice storms' when the heavy coating of ice may cause trees, telephone and electricity lines, poles and pylons to break, and bring great disruption over wide areas.

At about -37°C, water droplets freeze spontaneously, even in the absence of any freezing nuclei. Such freezing does occur occasionally very high in the atmosphere and gives rise to ice crystals that then fall and melt in the warmer lower layers, and may produce significant quantities of rain.

Heat and latent heat

Also important is the way in which water behaves with the addition or subtraction of heat. It takes heat to melt ice into liquid water, and still more heat to turn that liquid water into water vapour. In liquid water or vapour, that heat still exists in another form, when it is known as 'latent' (Latin: 'hidden') heat. When water vapour condenses into droplets or liquid water freezes into ice, that heat is released into the surroundings.

Although the evaporation of water – water turning into water vapour on heating or exposure to dry air – is familiar, the reverse process (condensation) also occurs, particularly when the temperature drops, with the water molecules either entering an open body of water, or else forming tiny droplets in the air or on cold objects. This is how fog or cloud droplets form.

Sublimation

When it comes to ice, quite apart from the processes by which liquid water freezes, and ice melts with the application of heat, it is also possible for water vapour to pass directly into ice or ice to turn into water vapour, without going through the intermediate stage of becoming liquid water. Solid ice may turn directly into water vapour in the process known as sublimation. This often occurs when an overnight frost (on plants or the ground) is exposed to sunlight, when the ice turns directly into water vapour.

The reverse process, where water vapour turns directly into solid ice is often also known as sublimation. To prevent confusion, in recent years the process has increasingly been called 'deposition'. This process (water vapour to ice) often occurs, for example, when branching 'feathers' of ice are deposited on greenhouse and conservatory glass panes: individual water molecules freeze onto pre-existing surfaces or particles of ice. The process is even more important (although invisible) high in the tops of certain clouds, where water molecules freeze onto ice crystals that have initially formed around freezing nuclei. The gradual growth of the ice crystals naturally causes them to become heavier and fall towards the ground. In many cases they then melt into raindrops.

Drying clothes on a freezing day

It is possible to take advantage of the sublimation process when drying clothes after washing. If wet clothes are hung out when the air temperature is below freezing, they will initially stiffen as hard as a board. But if the clothes are in sunshine, the ice will sublime, causing the water vapour to escape, and the clothes will be perfectly dry without going through a wet stage.

Air

Temperature variations in the air, and the way in which air moves are also important factors in the formation of clouds.

The change in air temperature with increasing height is known as the 'lapse rate'. An important point about the changes that occur as parcels of air rise and sink is that they take place without the addition or loss of heat. This condition is known as 'adiabatic' (Greek: 'impassible', implying neither the gaining nor the loss of heat).

Lapse rates

There are three, all-important lapse rates:

- **Dry Adiabatic Lapse Rate (DALR)** – The rate at which a parcel of air decreases in temperature as it rises in the atmosphere. Generally taken to be approximately 10 deg C per kilometre.
- **Environmental Lapse Rate (ELR)** – The actual rate at which temperature changes with height. This may be greater or less than the DALR, depending on the actual state of the atmosphere, and commonly varies in layers at different altitudes.
- **Saturated Adiabatic Lapse Rate (SALR)** – The rate at which a parcel of air decreases in temperature after condensation has set in. It is less than the DALR, because of the release of latent heat when the water vapour condenses into droplets of liquid water. It varies between approximately 4 and 7 deg C per kilometre, depending on the actual ambient temperatures involved. It is least at high temperatures, but greater at low temperatures, becoming similar to the DALR at about -40°C.

Stability and instability

Any parcel of air that is warmer than its surroundings is said to be unstable, and will tend to rise in the atmosphere. What happens when that parcel of air cools and cloud forms at the condensation point determines whether the parcel remains unstable and continues to ascend – giving rise to deeper cloud – or becomes stable, tending to remain at the same level. When condensation occurs (at a height known as the condensation level), latent heat (see page 22) is released and this may be enough to ensure that the parcel of air continues to rise. It will then do so at the SALR (the saturated lapse rate), which is less than the DALR (the dry lapse rate) that had applied as the parcel rose from the surface to the condensation level.

The release of latent heat at the condensation point may be a significant factor in the growth of clouds. Many cumulonimbus clouds (see page 37), for example, gain extra lift when the wind carries them over high ground, forcing additional condensation and the release of latent heat. That enables the thermals (see page 24) to continue rising, producing ever greater clouds.

On the other hand, air may sometimes be forced to rise – to flow over high ground, for example – and its temperature, decreasing at the DALR, becomes less than that of its surroundings. The air then tries to sink to a level at which its temperature is the same as surrounding air. In such a case, the air is said to be stable. Many layer clouds arise from such stable air.

Three ways in which clouds form

There are three basic ways in which clouds may form. All involve air rising in the atmosphere until it reaches a point at which the water vapour within it condenses into tiny cloud droplets, producing a cloud.

The three basic types of clouds, and the reasons for their formation are:

- **Convective clouds**– when parcels of warm air rise from the Earth's surface
- **Orographic clouds** – when air is forced to rise, perhaps when the wind encounters hills or mountains
- **Frontal clouds** – when air rises at the boundaries of different air masses with different temperatures

Convective clouds

Convective clouds arise when the surface is warmed by the Sun, and invisible 'bubbles' of warm air – known as 'thermals' – rise into the atmosphere. As

⬇ Convection bubbles of air occur when a film of warm air over a warm source (usually the ground) breaks free and begins to rise in the atmosphere. *(Ian Moores)*

the thermals rise, they expand, and become cooler. Such thermals will continue to rise all the time their temperature is higher than that of their surroundings. Eventually, they may reach the dewpoint (see page 20), at which the water vapour within them condenses into tiny droplets and a cloud is born. Such clouds frequently belong to the family of cumulus clouds. The way in which thermals rise from the surface is shown in the diagram below.

Orographic clouds

Orographic clouds are created when air is forced to rise because of features (such as hills or mountains) on the surface. The tops of hills or mountains are often shrouded in cloud that has formed in this way. To anyone on the high ground, they appear to be enveloped in mist or fog. Such clouds are often the type known as stratus, but

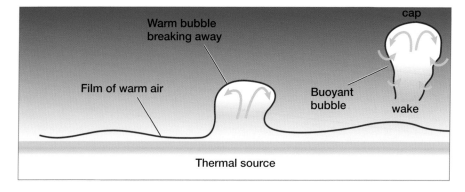

Warm bubble breaking away

cap

Film of warm air

Buoyant bubble

wake

Thermal source

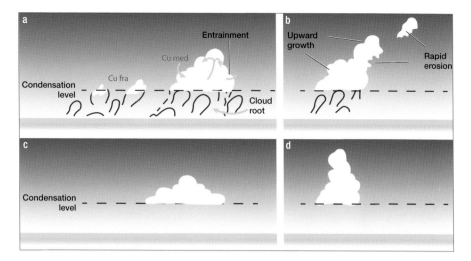

↑ Cumulus clouds appear when individual bubbles (or groups of bubbles) rise above the condensation level (a). Wind shear may cause them to dissipate rapidly (b). With low instability, the resulting clouds will be shallow (c), but with greater instability, considerable upward growth will occur (d). *(Ian Moores)*

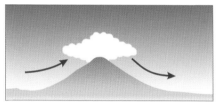

the lifting effect of the high ground may cause cumulus clouds to grow into the much greater cumulonimbus type. With stratiform clouds, frequently only the highest ground will be covered in cloud, because the cloud dissipates as the air descends on the leeward side of the hill or mountain.

↑ Air rising over high ground will, if it reaches the condensation level, shroud the heights in clouds, which will disperse as the air descends on the leeward side. *(Ian Moores)*

↓ Orographic Stratus clouds shrouding the mountains of South Georgia. *(Gordon Pedgrift)*

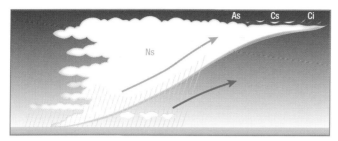

↑ A 'classic' warm front at which the warm air is rising over the whole frontal zone. For cloud type abbreviations, see page 37. *(Dominic Stickland)*

Frontal clouds

Frontal clouds arise when different air masses come into contact with one another. This most commonly occurs in depressions: low-pressure systems, that move across the globe and bring changeable weather to the surface. When a warm air mass meets a colder air mass, the warm air rises above the

Occluded front

In the later stages of the development of a depression system, the cold air mass may overtake the warm air, lifting it away from the surface. The resulting front in known as an occluded front, and its structure depends on whether the air ahead of, or behind the front is coldest. Either situation means that a pool of warm air is lifted away from the ground, and continues to give rain or snow, often for a long period of time.

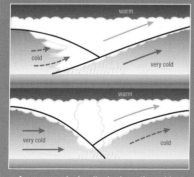

↑ A warm occlusion (top) where the coldest air is ahead of the front, and a cold occlusion (below) where the coldest air follows the front. *(Dominic Stickland)*

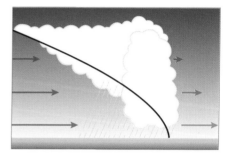

↑ A cold front where the cold air is undercutting the warm air and forcing it to rise. *(Dominic Stickland)*

↓ An approaching cold front on a comparitively rare occasion when there was little cloud in the warm sector, allowing a clear view of the front and its associated convective cloud. *(Author)*

colder air, and this then gives rise to cloud (and usually rain). Somewhat similarly, when a cold air mass catches up with a warm air mass, it tends to push beneath it, lifting the warm air away from the Earth's surface and again giving rise to cloud and rain.

'Special clouds'

Some forms of cloud are not derived directly from the usual meteorological processes, but by other natural forces or even by human activity. These are covered in the cloud classification scheme (see Chapter 3) by five special terms with the suffixes '-genitus' and '-mutatus', and are known by the overall term of 'Special Clouds'. The following forms of cloud are special clouds:

- **Cataractagenitus** – Waterfalls of all sizes may generate clouds of spray that persist in the form of mist, and the falling water tends to create an updraught that carries the spray upwards, where it may give rise to clouds, generally stratus fractus (see page 58) but which may develop further. Although the spray is usually confined to the immediate area of the waterfall, this mist may drift over neighbouring areas.

- **Flammagenitus** – This term applies to any clouds that form over a direct source of heat, such as a wildfire. Formerly, many such clouds were covered by the term 'pyrocumulus', but flammagenitus may be applied to forms other than cumulus.

- **Homogenitus** – This term is applied to any clouds that have formed through human activity. This includes clouds that have arisen over the cooling towers of power stations, as well as aircraft vapour trails (contrails).

- **Homomutatus** – This specifically applies to contrails that have changed over time. Contrails are often very persistent, and may be spread out by upper level winds to become broad bands of cloud.

- **Silvagenitus** – Large areas of trees may produce significant evaporation of water vapour into the air, giving rise to a general mist, which may be confined to the forested area, or drift over neighbouring regions.

↓ Dense cumulus congestus flamagenitus clouds looming above the smoke from a major wildfire in northern Florida. *(Durham Garbutt)*

↓ Persistent contrails slowly spreading across the sky in the humid, warm upper air, ahead of an approaching warm front. *(Author)*

Where clouds are formed

Clouds occur in three different regions of the atmosphere, known as the troposphere, the stratosphere and the mesosphere (see box opposite).

Although there are various ways in which atmospheric layers may be determined, the most significant method to meteorologists is a definition based on how the temperature changes with height.

There is one additional layer (defined by other characteristics) that is also recognised. This is the ionosphere, which extends over two of the other, outermost layers.

The three lowermost layers are of immediate interest in the study of clouds (although they are rare in the stratosphere and extremely rare in the mesosphere). Sometimes forms of the aurora (which occurs in the ionosphere) may initially be taken for clouds, but generally aurorae (see page 96) are very distinct, and are, of course, only seen at night.

Most of the clouds that concern us are found in the lowest layer, the troposphere (from Greek, meaning 'sphere of change'), where nearly all weather originates. Other, rarer clouds are found in the next-highest layer, the stratosphere, and some very unusual clouds occur even higher, in the layer known as the mesosphere. We can begin with the lowest layer, troposphere, and work upwards.

Clouds in the troposphere

The troposphere is the layer of the atmosphere that is closest to the Earth.

- Within the troposphere, the temperature generally falls with increasing height, up to the top of the layer, which is known as the tropopause. (Above this level, the temperature starts to rise, in the stratosphere.)
- Because the troposphere is deeper in the tropics (around 15–18km) than it is at the poles (around 8km), clouds may grow much higher close to the equator than they do when farther north or south.
- Between the ground and the tropopause, the overall decline in temperature is about 6.5 deg C per km. (So the lowest temperatures often occur at the equatorial tropopause.) The rate of decline fluctuates and may sometimes be as high as 10 deg C per km, or may even increase over a limited range of heights in what is known as an inversion.

⬇ Typical tropospheric cumulus clouds. *(Author)*

The layers and boundaries in the atmosphere

The following tables show the various layers and boundaries in the atmosphere and the heights which they occupy.

Note: *The variation in base heights is caused by specific meteorological conditions, the latitude and the seasons of the year.*

ATMOSPHERIC LAYERS

Layer name	Base height above ground	Top height above ground
Troposphere	Earth's surface	8km to 15–18km
Stratosphere	8km to 15–18km	50km
Mesosphere	50km	80–95km to 100–120km
Thermosphere	80–95km	200–700km
Exosphere	Above 200–700km	Interplanetary space
Ionosphere	60–70km	1,000km or more

The boundaries between the various layers have specific names (named after the underlying layer) as shown in this table. When it comes to clouds, just two (the tropopause and the mesopause) are of particular significance.

ATMOSPHERIC BOUNDARIES

Boundary name	Height above ground
Tropopause	Approximately 15–18km at the equator Approximately 8km at the poles
Stratopause	50km
Mesopause	80–95km during winter 100–120km during summer at the poles
Thermopause	200–700km

➜ The layers in the atmosphere. *(Ian Moores)*

Clouds in the stratosphere

The stratosphere is marked by the fact that within it, the temperature increases with height.

■ Sometimes the region immediately above the tropopause maintains a constant temperature for some kilometres as the height increases (in what is known as an isothermal layer), but overall the temperature increases up to the top of the stratosphere (the stratopause) at about 50km altitude. This increase is because of the absorption of heat by the chemical reactions that create ozone in the upper region. The ozone layer plays an important role, because it shields the surface and its lifeforms from the damaging effects of ultraviolet radiation from the Sun.

■ A few clouds occur in the stratosphere. Sometimes cumulonimbus clouds (see page 82) are so vigorous that they overshoot the tropopause and penetrate a short distance above it. Otherwise, clouds in the stratosphere are limited to the very lowest (and coldest) region and may include some cirrus (see page 74), and the uncommon, but very striking, mother-of-pearl clouds (see page 90).

Clouds in the mesosphere

Meteorologists recognise three additional layers above the stratosphere: the mesosphere, the thermosphere, and the exosphere.

■ As mentioned earlier, the ionosphere consists of portions of the mesosphere and exosphere. The only region that concerns us at present is the

→ Noctilucent clouds photographed from Scotland
(Denis Buczynski)

mesosphere, because the very highest clouds of all (noctilucent clouds, see page 92) occur far above all other clouds at heights of at least 85 kilometres.

■ Above the stratopause at about an altitude of about 50 km, the temperature begins to drop dramatically, reaching the atmospheric minimum of between –163°C and –100°C at the top of the layer (the mesopause).

■ The mesopause tends to occur at two distinct levels around 86km and around 100km, with the highest level being found towards the poles in summer.

The mysterious upper atmosphere

Very little is known about the higher layers of the atmosphere, such as the strength and direction of the winds, even though it is now suspected that these layers – contrary to earlier beliefs – do exert some influence on the weather occurring far below. The layers are too high to be reached easily by research balloons. The standard meteorological instruments that are released regularly to obtain atmospheric measurements tend to reach altitudes of just 20–25km before the 'met balloons' carrying them burst. So they reach the tropopause and the lower stratosphere. Some special research balloons are designed to rise higher, but 40km is about the limit. The lowest meteorological and environmental satellites orbit at altitudes of a few hundred kilometres, so there is a vast region of the atmosphere that is essentially unobserved (although unmanned drones are currently being developed to fly in the upper atmosphere). Because this high-altitude region and its winds are so poorly studied, any observations of the noctilucent clouds (see page 92) that do occur in the mesosphere, and their changes, are of considerable scientific interest. Occasionally, some research rockets release chemicals that may be tracked from the ground, and sometimes the exhaust plumes from rocket launches provide similar information about high-altitude winds.

→ Not a nacreous cloud, but the result of a missile launch from Vandenberg Air Force Base in California, and where water vapour from the exhaust has frozen into ice. The distortions in the trail are an indication of differing wind directions at various heights.
(Stephen Pitt)

The Cloud

By Percy Bysshe Shelley

I bring fresh showers for the thirsting flowers,
From the seas and the streams;
I bear light shade for the leaves when laid
In their noonday dreams.
From my wings are shaken the dews that waken
The sweet buds every one,
When rocked to rest on their mother's breast,
As she dances about the sun.
I wield the flail of the lashing hail,
And whiten the green plains under,
And then again I dissolve it in rain,
And laugh as I pass in thunder.

Chapter 3
Cloud classification

As explained in Chapter 1, Luke Howard proposed a formal classification of clouds which was published in 1803 and was widely accepted. His classification scheme was successful because he recognised (and allowed for) changes in the form and structure of clouds, and some of his terms remain in use today.

← Lenticular clouds formed over Mount Shasta in California.
(Shutterstock)

The naming of clouds

Although Luke Howard described just a few basic forms of cloud and introduced names for them, even he found that he needed to extend his naming scheme to cope with the changes that occur in clouds.

The formal classification, as established by the World Meteorological Organisation (WMO), seems at first sight to be quite complicated. In reality, it describes clouds in a very rational way, and it is usually easy enough to come to recognise the different terms. The scheme described here is the 'official' set of terms established by the WMO and published in their *International Cloud Atlas*. Some broader classes, occasionally used to describe clouds are also mentioned.

The main classification scheme is described in this chapter. Details and illustrations of the individual types of

clouds, their species, varieties and other characteristics are covered in Chapter 3. The ways in which clouds are formed and details of where they occur are provided in Chapter 4.

The way in which the full classification describes clouds may seem complicated, but there are definite, logical reasons for the various sub-divisions and for the terms that are used. Most animals and plants are described in the Linnaean system – introduced by Carl Linnaeus (1707–1778) – with a double Latin name: A genus (or type) and a species. Examples of terms used for the genus (plural is genera) of animals and

⬇ The skull of *Homo Neanderthalensis*. *(Wikipedia)*

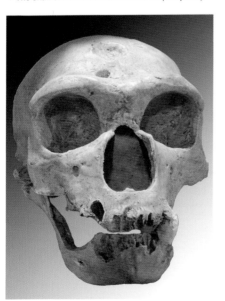

⬇ *Pinus nigra* (the black pine). *(Wikipedia)*

plants are: *Homo* for all humans (particularly for the group known nowadays as 'hominins'), and *Pinus* for any form of pine tree. When it comes to species, we may have *Homo neanderthalensis* or *Homo sapiens* for two different types of human, and perhaps *Pinus radiata* for the Monterey pine, or *Pinus nigra*, for the Austrian or black pine. Linnaeus introduced this classification scheme for plants in 1753 and for animals in 1758.

With clouds, we might, for example, have *Cumulus* (a heaped cloud) as a cloud genus, and *Cumulus mediocris*, or 'medium cumulus', as genus and species. For some clouds, in addition to the terms for genus and species, yet a third term (variety) is sometimes used to describe the transparency and the arrangement of individual cloud elements. We might, for example, have *Cumulus humilis radiatus* for shallow cumulus in rows. Of course, there may be more than one type of cloud present in the sky at any one time, but it is

↑ Cumulus mediocris. *(Author)*

usually easy enough to distinguish between them. Clouds do change their nature and sometimes they evolve into a different type. There are usually specific reasons and conditions that cause this to happen, and some instances are mentioned later. Standardised

↓ Cumulus humilis radiatus. *(Author)*

abbreviations are used for all the various terms.

One complaint that is sometimes made is that the Latin names of clouds are difficult to remember. Unfortunately, because Latin is less commonly understood nowadays, and it is no longer generally taught in schools, many people do have some difficulty in remembering (or pronouncing) the names of clouds. There are just ten main cloud types, however, so it should not be too difficult to remember those. Although Howard's scheme has been greatly modified in the years since it was first devised, Latin words are still used for the many sub-types of cloud that are now recognised. Some knowledge of Latin does help to remember the specific features after which many of the individual sub-classes are named, so a brief description of each term is given when it is first introduced in this book.

So the overall scheme for classifying clouds has the following basic terms:

- **Genus (plural is genera)** – Ten main terms (two-letter abbreviations), describing the overall characteristics.
- **Species** – Fifteen terms (three-letter abbreviations), describing cloud shape and structure. Some cloud types (genera) occur as just a single species. Many species apply to more than one genus.
- **Variety** – Nine terms (two-letter abbreviations), that describe the transparency or arrangement of individual cloud elements. Sometimes more than one variety is applied to individual cloud-forms.

This may all seem complicated enough, but there are some additional terms that are used. However, do not despair; these terms are very descriptive and easily recognised when they apply to actual clouds. There are two groups: 'supplementary features' and 'accessory clouds'.

- **Supplementary features** – Ten terms (three-letter abbreviations) describing particular forms of cloud.
- **Accessory clouds** – Four terms (three-letter abbreviations) for minor cloud forms that occur only in association with one of the main cloud genera.

There are two other terms that are sometimes used. These take the form of suffixes that are added to the names of a particular cloud genus, and indicate the way in which the observed cloud has been formed. These two terms are '-genitus' (abbreviated 'gen') and '-mutatus' (abbreviated 'mut'). The first indicates that significant amounts of the parent cloud are still present, whereas the second indicates that essentially all of the parent cloud has been altered.

At the time of writing, the latest edition of the *International Cloud Atlas* has also introduced five '-genitus' and '-mutatus' terms that describe specific ways in which particular clouds (known as 'special clouds') have formed.

All these cloud forms and the significance of their names are more fully described elsewhere in this book. The appropriate pages are shown in the summary tables given below. Also shown are the cloud genera to which the various sub-classes generally apply. Examples of one form from each group are shown, but more extensively illustrated later.

Cloud genus (plural, genera)

Ten basic cloud types describing the major, overall characteristics: two-letter abbreviations.

Genus	Abbr.	Description	Page
altocumulus	Ac	Heaps or rolls of cloud, showing distinct shading, and with clear gaps between them, in a layer at middle levels	67
altostratus	As	Sheet of featureless, white or grey cloud at middle levels	64
cirrocumulus	Cc	Tiny heaps of cloud with no shading, with clear gaps, in a layer at high levels	79
cirrostratus	Cs	Essentially featureless sheet of thin cloud at high levels	77
cirrus	Ci	Fibrous wisps of cloud at high levels	74
cumulonimbus	Cb	Large towering cloud extending to great heights, with ragged base and heavy precipitation	82
cumulus	Cu	Rounded heaps of cloud at low levels	50
nimbostratus	Ns	Dark grey cloud at middle levels, frequently extending down towards the Earth's surface, and giving prolonged precipitation	72
stratocumulus	Sc	Heaps or rolls of cloud, with distinct gaps and heavy shading at low levels	59
stratus	St	Essentially featureless, grey layer cloud at low level	56

➜ Altocumulus floccus.
(Author)

Cloud species

Fifteen terms to describe cloud shape and structure: three-letter abbreviations.

Species	Abbr.	Description	Genera	Page
calvus	cal	Tops of rising cells lose their hard appearance and become smooth	Cb	84
capillatus	cap	Tops of rising cells become distinctly fibrous or streaked; obvious cirrus may appear	Cb	85
castellanus	cas	Distinct turrets rising from an extended base or line of cloud	Sc, Ac, Cc, Ci	62, 69, 80, 75
congestus	con	Great vertical extent; obviously growing vigorously, with hard, 'cauliflower-like' tops	Cu	53
fibratus	fib	Fibrous appearance, normally straight or uniformly curved; no distinct hooks	Ci, Cs	76, 79
floccus	flo	Individual tufts of cloud, with ragged bases, sometimes with distinct virga	Sc, Ac, Cc, Ci	69, 76, 80
fractus	fra	Broken cloud with ragged edges and base	Cu, St	52, 58
humilis	hum	Cloud of restricted vertical extent; length much greater than height	Cu	52
lenticularis	len	Lens- or almond-shaped clouds, stationary in the sky	Sc, Ac, Cc	62, 69, 80
mediocris	med	Cloud of moderate vertical extent, growing upwards	Cu	53
nebulosus	neb	Featureless sheet of cloud, with no structure	St, Cs	58, 79
spissatus	spi	Dense cloud, appearing grey when viewed towards the Sun	Ci	76
stratiformis	str	Cloud in an extensive sheet or layer	Sc, Ac, Cc	62, 71, 81
uncinus	unc	Distinctly hooked, often without a visible generating head	Ci	76
volutus	vol	A tubular cloud, sometimes appearing to roll	Sc, (rarely Ac)	

← Altocumulus lenticularis, generated in the crests of wave motion created by distant hills. *(Author)*

→ Cumulus cloud streets (cumulus radiatus), streaming eastwards on a westerly wind, with jet-stream cirrus above. *(Author)*

Cloud varieties

Nine terms that describe cloud transparency and the arrangement of the individual cloud elements: two-letter abbreviations. Any particular cloud may exhibit the characteristics of more than one variety – often several may be present simultaneously.

Variety	Abbr.	Description	Genera	Page
duplicatus	du	Two or more layers	Sc, Ac, Ci, Cs	62, 71, 76, 79
intortus	in	Tangled or irregularly curved	Ci	76
lacunosus	la	Thin cloud with regularly spaced holes, appearing like a net	Ac, Cc, Sc	62, 71, 81
opacus	op	Thick cloud that completely hides Sun or Moon	St, Sc, Ac, As	58, 63, 66, 72
perlucidus	pe	Extensive layer with gaps, through which blue sky, the Sun or Moon are visible	Sc, Ac	63, 72
radiatus	ra	Appearing to radiate from one point in the sky	Cu, Sc, Ac, As, Ci	54, 63, 66, 72, 76
translucidus	tr	Translucent cloud, through which the position of the Sun or Moon is readily visible	St, Sc, Ac, As	59, 63, 66, 72
undulatus	un	Layer or patch of cloud with distinct undulations	St, Sc, Ac, As, Cc, Cs	59, 63, 66, 72, 79, 81
vertebratus	ve	Lines of cloud looking like ribs, vertebrae or fish bones	Ci	76

Accessory clouds

Four forms that occur only in conjunction with specific types of the 10 main genera: three-letter abbreviations.

Name	Abbr.	Description	Genera	Page
flumen	flm	Low band of cloud flowing in towards a supercell	Cb	86
pannus	pan	Ragged shreds beneath main cloud mass	Cu, Cb, As, Ns	86
pileus	pil	Hood or cap of cloud above rising cell	Cu, Cb	86
velum	vel	Thin, extensive sheet of cloud, through which the most vigorous cells may penetrate	Cu, Cb	86

↑ Pannus beneath nimbostratus. *(Author)*

→ Cirrus homogenitus. *(Author)*

↓ Cavum in a sheet of altocumulus. *(Author)*

Supplementary features

Eleven particular forms (some common, others quite rare) that particular genera or species may adopt: three-letter abbreviations.

Feature	Abbr.	Description	Genera	Page
arcus	arc	Arch or roll of cloud	Cb, Cu	87
asperitas	asp	Wave-like features on the underside of clouds	Sc, Ac	89
cauda	cau	Horizontal, tail-shaped cloud, extending towards murus	Cb (supercell)	87
cavum	cav	An approximately circular (or linear) hole in a layer of cloud	Ac, Cc (rarely Sc)	89
fluctus	flu	Short-lived 'breaking' waves or curls on the top of clouds	Ci, Ac, Sc, St (rarely Cu)	89
incus	inc	Anvil cloud	Cb	87
mamma	mam	Bulges or pouches beneath higher cloud	Cb, Ci, Cc, Ac, As, Sc	87
murus	mur	Abrupt, localised lowering of cloud	Cb	88
praecipitatio	pre	Precipitation that reaches the surface	Cb, Cu, Ns	88
tuba	tub	Funnel cloud of any type	Cb, Cu	88
virga	vir	Fallstreaks: trails of precipitation that do not reach the surface	Ac, As, Cc, Cb, Cu, Ns, Sc, (Ci)	88

Special clouds

Term	Description	Examples	Page
flammagenitus	Clouds that develop over a heat source	Cu, Cb	27
homogenitus	Clouds created by human activity	Ci, Cu	27
homomutatus	Contrails that have changed form over time	Ci	27
cataracagenitus	Clouds created near a large waterfall	Cu, St	27
silvagenitus	Clouds that develop over forests	St	27

Classifying clouds by appearance

Sometimes clouds are divided into two broad categories based on their overall appearance – cumuliform and stratiform.

Cumuliform clouds are heaped clouds, or clouds occurring in distinct heaps, rolls, or 'pancakes':

- Cumulus (Cu)
- Stratocumulus (Sc)
- Altocumulus (Ac)
- Cirrocumulus (Cc)
- Cumulonimbus (Cb)

Stratiform clouds occur as distinct layers:

- Stratus
- Nimbostratus
- Altostratus
- Cirrostratus

However, it should be noted that stratocumulus, altocumulus and cirrocumulus usually occur within a distinct layer, so they could be considered to show both cumuliform and stratiform characteristics. One genus, cirrus, does not fit easily into either category. Although some cloud forms, for example, altostratus, often consist of a mixture of water droplets and ice crystals, it is sometimes useful to distinguish clouds that contain just ice crystals, when these are known as 'cirriform' clouds:

- Cirrus
- Cirrocumulus
- Cirrostratus

⬇ The Tuscan sky filled with cumuliform cloud. *(Carole Tyrell)*

⬆ A sheet of stratiform cloud over Venice. *(Carole Tyrell)* ⬇ Extensive cirriform cloud. *(Author)*

Classifying clouds by height

Another way of classifying clouds is by their height – the level at which they occur in the atmosphere. There is a whole, extremely detailed, technical classification scheme based on height, with numerical sub-divisions for individual forms, intended for official observers.

The altitude of clouds is generally difficult for amateur observers to determine, which means that classifying clouds by their height is more difficult, so the scheme is not covered in detail here. Clouds are considered to occur within three height ranges, or levels. Previously these three height ranges were known by the term 'étage', and this will be found in many older books.

When discussing clouds, some terms relating to height have been given specific meanings to prevent confusion. These are:

- **Altitude** – The height above sea level.
- **Height** – The altitude of cloudbase above an observing site or other location, such as an airfield, but often specified as above mean sea level.

- **Vertical height (or depth)** – The distance from the base of a cloud to its top.

The altitudes of the main cloud genera have been found by observation to lie between sea level and 18km (60,000ft) in the tropics, approximately 13km (45,000ft) at middle latitudes, and up to 8km (25,000ft) in the polar regions. This does not apply to the two, relatively rare, higher forms: nacreous clouds (see page 90) and noctilucent clouds (see page 92).

When clouds are grouped by height, the lower atmosphere, in which most clouds occur, is divided into three height ranges, known as levels: high, medium and low. (The designations C_H, C_M, and C_L are used for these levels in technical observational reports.) The levels are actually defined by the range of altitudes at which certain specific cloud genera generally occur. The genera used in the definitions are:

- High
  - Cirrus (Ci)
  - Cirrocumulus (Cc)
  - Cirrostratus (Cs)
- Medium
  - Altocumulus (Ac)
- Low
  - Stratus (St)
  - Stratocumulus (Sc)

Why are cloud heights given in feet?

Cloud heights are frequently given in feet, rather than in a metric measurement (although SI equivalents are often given). This is because, many years ago, the aviation industry standardised on the use of feet for the height of aircraft and the height of clouds is obviously extremely relevant for aviation.

Note that certain genera are not included among those used to define the three levels. This is because those particular cloud types may cover a range of altitudes:

■ **Altostratus** – is normally regarded as a middle-level cloud, but may extend upwards into the high level.
■ **Nimbostratus** – is likewise usually discussed as a middle-level cloud, but often extends to higher and lower levels.
■ **Both cumulus and cumulonimbus** – are regarded as low-level clouds because of the altitude of their bases, but they often have great vertical extent, reaching the middle and high levels. Cumulonimbus clouds, in particular, frequently grow through all three levels,

↑ This photograph taken from the Intenational Space Station over western Africa shows Cumulonimbus clouds reaching up to the tropopause at an altitude of about 15km. All significant weather is confined to the troposphere, the layer below that height. *(NASA)*

reaching the tropopause, and may even overshoot it slightly.

The various levels actually tend to overlap and their altitudes vary with latitude. The approximate altitudes are shown in the table below and the maximum altitudes at each latitude are those of the atmospheric boundary known as the tropopause (see page 29), below which almost all clouds and weather occur.

Altitude ranges of high, medium and low clouds

Level	Tropical regions	Temperate regions	Polar regions
High	6–18km (20,000–60,000ft)	5–13km (16,000–45,000ft)	3–8km (10,000–25,000ft)
Medium	2–8km (6,500–25,000ft)	2–7km (6,500–23,000ft)	2–4km (6,500–13,000ft)
Low	Surface to 2km (6,500ft)	Surface to 2km (6,500ft)	Surface to 2km (6,500ft)

"Clouds come floating into my life, no longer to carry rain or usher storm, but to add colour to my sunset sky."

Rabindranath Tagore, *Stray Birds* (1916)

Chapter 4

Cloud identification

There are so many different types of
cloud, and several may occur in the sky at
any one time, so it is often difficult to
determine exactly which cloud forms are
visible. This chapter will help you to
identify the clouds you see.

← Cumulus cloud appearing dark againt the setting Sun, with
cirrus high overhead. *(Shutterstock)*

Cloud identification flow chart

This flowchart shows the most common cloud forms, and should help you to make a start on identifying what you can see. The various forms of cloud are more fully described on the following pages. The page numbers shown here will provide more information about all the numerous cloud types, species and varieties that may occur.

The overall classification of clouds was discussed in Chapter 3, and the way in which clouds are formed is explained in Chapter 2.

| 1 | Are the clouds separate individual clumps rather than an extensive layer? | Yes | Go to 3 |
| | | No | Go to 7 |

| 2 | Are the clouds heavy with an anvil-shaped top? | Yes | Go to Cumulonimbus (page 82) |
| | | No | Go to cumulus (page 50) |

| 3 | Are the clouds shaped like cauliflowers? | Yes | Go to 2 |
| | | No | Go to 8 |

| 4 | Is the cloud rippled? | Yes | Go to Ac un (page 72) |
| | | No | Go to 5 |

| 5 | Is the cloud lens-shaped? | Yes | Go to Ac len (page 69) |
| | | No | Go to 6 |

| 6 | Do the clouds show upward turrets? | Yes | Go to Ac cas (page 69) |
| | | No | Go to Ac (page 67) |

| 7 | Are the clouds in small patches? | Yes | Go to 4 |
| | | No | Go to 12 |

| 8 | Are the clouds very high and delicate? | Yes | Go to 6 |
| | | No | Go to 7 |

| 9 | Are the clouds in tiny tufts? | Yes | Go to Cc (page 79) |
| | | No | Go to 10 |

| 10 | Are the clouds hooked? | Yes | Go to Ci unc (page 76) |
| | | No | Go to 11 |

| 11 | Is the cloud in long lines? | Yes | Go to homomutatus (page 27) |
| | | No | Go to Ci (page 74) |

| 12 | Is the layer patchy? | Yes | Go to Sc (page 59) |
| | | No | Go to 14 |

| 13 | Does the Sun still cast shadows? | Yes | Go to Cs (page 77) |
| | | No | Go to As (page 64) |

| 14 | Is Sun visible through cloud? | Yes | Go to 13 |
| | | No | Go to 15 |

| 15 | Light drizzle or heavier rain? | Yes | Go to St (page 56) |
| | | No | Go to Ns (page 72) |

Low-level clouds

Low-level clouds are defined as those with bases below 2km (approx. 6,600ft) above the Earth's surface. Note, however that cumulonimbus clouds also often have their bases at about 2km, but may extend throughout the whole depth of the troposphere. For this reason, they are usually considered separately.

The three main genera of low clouds are:
- Cumulus (C)
- Stratus (St)
- Stratocumulus (Sc)

Cumulus (Cu)

Cumulus clouds are the 'fair-weather' clouds, with flat bases and rounded tops – often the 'default' clouds drawn by children.

Cumulus clouds are the visible signs of thermals arising from a warm surface. The Earth's surface layer is heated by sunlight, and eventually 'bubbles' of warm air break away from the surface and begin to rise (see illustration on page 24). Once these parcels of warm air rise, they begin to incorporate cooler air from their surroundings. They may however, rise sufficiently, cooling as they do so, until they reach a level at which the water vapour within them condenses into tiny droplets and a cloud is born. The result is that the bases of cumulus clouds all lie at about the same level, and this is usually clearly apparent when several clouds are visible in the sky.

All cumulus clouds are water-droplet clouds, and most of them do not produce any rain. An indication of this is the fact that their bases are flat. When clouds produce precipitation, whether that be rain, snow or even hail, their bases become uneven – ragged. One species, cumulus congestus (described later) is a major source of rain in the tropics and often gives rise to rain in temperate regions in summer, when it may grow to become extremely deep.

⬇ **Cumulus clouds.** *(Author)*

Summer clouds

In general, the cloudbase is higher in summer than in winter. This is because the environment (the surrounding air) is usually warmer and drier, so the thermals must ascend farther for them to cool sufficiently for condensation to occur. In summer, it is often noticeable that cloudbase is higher in the afternoon than in the early morning.

THE EVOLUTION OF CUMULUS CLOUDS

Cumulus (Cu) clouds may evolve from:

- Stratus (St)
- Stratocumulus (Sc)
- Altocumulus (Ac)

Although cumulus clouds often arise from thermals, they may also derive from the erosion of other cloud types. What begins the day as a sheet of stratus (particularly over land) may gradually rise as heating from the Sun takes place and become a sheet of stratocumulus, with individual rolls or pancakes of cloud, separated by narrow gaps. The process may continue with the stratocumulus layer breaking up completely into individual sections and these go on to become cumulus clouds. A somewhat similar process may occasionally occur with a higher altocumulus layer, although it is not often that the result may be described as true cumulus, rather than altocumulus. True cumulus clouds show signs of upward growth – seen in their rounded tops – which is a sign that the atmosphere in that layer is unstable (see page 59).

Cumulus (Cu) clouds may evolve into:

- Stratocumulus (Sc)
- Altocumulus (Ac)
- Cumulonimbus (Cb)

The lifecycle of a cumulus cloud

Early in the day, the thermals tend to be fairly small and weak, and rapidly mix with their surroundings. Any wind will easily disperse them, and as a result, the cloud droplets are easily dispersed and rapidly evaporate. For this reason, early in the day, cumulus clouds are small and ragged (cumulus fractus), and short-lived. As the day progresses, and the thermals become stronger, the resulting clouds become larger and tend to persist. Generally, the heaps of cloud remain distinct and separate from one another, even as they increase in size.

Generally, the rounded tops of cumulus clouds show that they are actively growing upwards. When this growth ceases, for example towards the end of a day, when the Sun's heat fades, the number of clouds begins to decrease, and the individual clouds start to decay, becoming ragged and finally evaporating into the surrounding air. So cumulus clouds start life as ragged wisps and end their lives in a similar form.

Cumulus clouds often cease to rise when they reach a temperature inversion, where temperature increases with height. They then tend to spread sideways, forming a blanket of cloud, and becoming a sheet of stratocumulus or, if higher, altocumulus. Under different conditions, when there is great heating, cumulus may grow extensively, passing through the species known as cumulus mediocris and cumulus congestus (described in the following section) to become massive cumulonimbus clouds. These are shower clouds, with very distinct characteristics, which are described later. Individual cumulus cells tend to cluster together to give rise to these giant clouds.

SPECIES OF CUMULUS CLOUD

There are four distinct species (see page 38) of cumulus clouds:

- Cumulus fractus (Cu fra)
- Cumulus humilis (Cu hum)
- Cumulus mediocris (Cu med)
- Cumulus congestus (Cu con)

Cumulus fractus (Cu fra) are often no more than misty patches in the air early in the day. These usually become small,

distinct clouds, which change rapidly and continuously. Because they are produced by rising thermals, they often show a roughly domed top, even though they are little more than wisps of cloud. At the end of the day, when heating from the Sun dies away, cumulus clouds dissipate, gradually eroding and becoming ragged with little distinct shape. Again, these are cumulus fractus, so cumulus clouds begin and end as cumulus fractus.

Cumulus humilis (Cu hum) are very shallow clouds, with bases that are much wider than the clouds' vertical depth. The tops are very gently rounded, but often display a distinctly flattened appearance. This frequently occurs early in the day, when the clouds have only just started their growth and begin to change from their initial cumulus fractus form. If they continue to grow, they will become cumulus mediocris. Cumulus humilis clouds are often seen ahead of an advancing warm front, where the invading warm air at altitude creates an inversion that limits the upward growth of cumulus clouds beneath it. At the same time, high cloud (such as cirrostratus, page 77) tends

⬇ Cumulus fractus. *(Author)*

⬇ Cumulus humilis. *(Author)*

↑ Cumulus mediocris, leaning downwind.
(Judy Darley)

↑ Summertime cumulus congestus. (Author)

to limit the radiation reaching the ground and so limits heating of the surface, cutting off the supply of heat and weakening the consequent thermals. Both causes limit the upward growth of the cumulus clouds, leading to an increase in cumulus humilis.

Cumulus mediocris (Cu med) are large cumulus clouds. The individual clouds show distinct signs of upward growth, with normally small, but clearly defined, rounded bulges to the tops of the clouds. The overall appearance may be approximately triangular, where one part of the cloud (usually the centre) is distinctly higher than the other regions. The overall depth of the clouds may be slightly less or approximately equal to the width of the base. If the wind is strong, there may be considerable vertical wind shear – a difference in wind strength or direction with

height – and the clouds may seem to 'lean' downwind, although this feature may be much more marked in the next, large species, cumulus congestus.

Cumulus congestus (Cu con), sometimes called 'towering cumulus' are formed when cumulus clouds grow very vigorously, their height often becoming much greater than the width of their base. The tops of the rising cells usually appear brilliantly white, and generally appear 'bumpy', resembling the head of a cauliflower. These tops appear sharp, and show no signs of being fibrous or having a streaked structure. This is an indication that the tops have not become glaciated – ie, that the cloud particles have not turned to ice crystals. However, the tops may fray out slightly when they decay, but never become wispy like cirrus clouds. When

Cumulus congestus (Cu con) and the weather

The currents within cumulus congestus are very vigorous, and (especially in summer in temperate regions, or at any time of year in the tropics) they may grow sufficiently deep to produce rain. The turbulence and great depth enable the tiny cloud droplets to collide with one another (which does not happen in most cumulus clouds) and produce what meteorologists describe as 'warm rain' (see page 113 for details of 'warm' and 'cold' rain).

When rain falls from cumulus congestus it is normally in the form of a short shower. When such a cloud is overhead and producing rain, it may be mistaken for altostratus or nimbostratus, but these types of cloud generally produce more prolonged periods of rain, although usually light from altostratus cloud. There is an even greater likelihood of confusion with a cumulonimbus cloud, because cumulonimbus actually develop from cumulus congestus. The distinctive features of cumulonimbus clouds are described on page 84. By convention, if none of the distinctive features of a cumulonimbus (such as an anvil or plume of cirrus cloud) are visible, and neither is there any hail or associated lightning and thunder, the cloud is considered to be cumulus congestus.

there is strong vertical wind shear the whole cloud may 'lean' downwind, sometimes at a considerable angle.

VARIETY OF CUMULUS CLOUD

There is just one variety (see Chapter 3) of cumulus. This is **cumulus radiatus (Cu ra)**, where clouds are arranged in distinct lines. These are known as 'cloud streets' and are reasonably common. They are often seen in satellite images, especially where cold air is streaming off land and out over a warm sea. The most common species are cumulus humilis radiatus (Cu hum ra) and cumulus mediocris radiatus (Cu med ra).

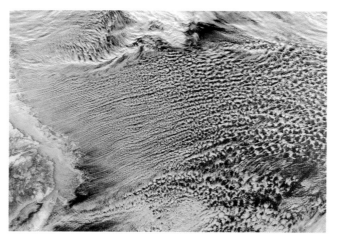

← Cloud streets over the cold waters of the Labrador Sea. *(NASA)*

'Cloud streets'

When cumulus radiatus (Cu ra) is visible, as 'cloud streets', sometimes there may be a single line of cloud, such as shown in the image on page 35, but on other occasions there may be a whole series of parallel lines of cloud, covering a wide area. Because of the way in which solar heating affects the ground, particular patches may become much warmer than the surrounding area and act as a source of thermals. These may then be carried downwind and give rise to a line of cloud.

The most favourable conditions for clouds streets to occur are when the lowest layer of air is unstable through heating of the surface (convection), but the growth of the thermals is limited because the layer is capped by an inversion, where the

↑ Cloud streets (cumulus humilis radiatus) with jet-stream cirrus above. *(Author)*

temperature increases with height. Air rises in the thermals (producing the clouds), and sinks more gently in the clear spaces between the lines. The spacing between the lines of cloud tends to be twice or three times the depth of the lowermost (unstable) layer. For cloud streets to persist, the convection should be fairly weak. If stronger, the cloud may simply spread out beneath the inversion, becoming a layer of stratocumulus. With even stronger convection, thermals may even break through the inversion, causing cloud growth to become more chaotic and for the cloud streets to disappear.

Stratus (St)

Stratus is a very familiar cloud, although one that has few distinguishing features. It is a low, grey or blue-grey blanket of water-droplet cloud. It often hides the top of high buildings and hills and mountains, but its base may often descend to ground level, when it forms mist or fog. Its base is soft, rather than ragged and there is little or no precipitation.

Stratus is the lowest cloud type. Rarely is its base higher than 500m (about 1,600ft). There is no difference between stratus and fog: just the fact that the base of stratus is above the ground. The density of stratus is usually fairly uniform, but its transparency may vary considerably, from being so thin (in the stratus translucidus variety) that the outline of the Sun or Moon is visible through it, to being so dense that they are completely invisible (in the stratus opacus variety – which may appear dark, blue-grey and very 'heavy').

The base of stratus is normally reasonably well-defined, although it may appear soft when observed from close by, and it may show distinct undulations . It

⬇ Heavy stratus cloud. *(Author)*

may occur as a continuous layer covering the whole sky, or occur in distinct patches. The top of the layer, when seen from a mountain-top or aircraft, is usually fairly smooth and featureless.

THE EVOLUTION OF STRATUS CLOUDS

Stratus (St) normally forms when moist air travels over a cold surface. If there is little wind, and resulting turbulence, the layer of cloud hugs the ground in the form of fog. With a slightly stronger wind, stratus cloud forms at the top of the mixed layer of air, and may spread down towards the surface. Generally, if the wind is strong,

little cloud forms, because mixing occurs within a very deep layer of air.

When conditions are fairly still, stratus may be confined to just a thin layer, and the tops of hills and mountains may be in bright sunshine above the layer of cloud. With stronger winds, however, moist air is often forced to rise over high ground, resulting in the hill-tops becoming shrouded in cloud (appearing as mist or fog to anyone within it), while neighbouring low-lying ground is fog free.

If there is a great difference in temperature between the air and the surface, stratus may still be produced. It is such a large temperature difference that leads to the notorious 'Force 10 fog' that sometimes occurs over the Shetlands.

Stratus clouds may evolve from:
- Fog
- Stratocumulus (Sc)

After fog has formed overnight, it may begin to lift in the morning as heat from the Sun starts to warm the ground. The fog tends to rise and becomes a low stratus layer. This may often be seen lying along river valleys and in similar situations

⬆ A layer of stratus, risen from low-lying fog over the Straits of Magellan in Patagonia. *(Francis Bell)*

near coastlines. Generally, the layer continues to break up, especially if the wind rises, giving rise to patches of broken cloud, and these are sometime seen to rise up the sides of hills and mountains. (They are known as 'call boys' in certain parts of the country, particularly in Sussex.)

Occasionally, stratus may develop from stratocumulus, particularly when the shallow convection, which creates the structure of individual cloudlets, ceases. The layer becomes indistinct, losing its structure and the base may lower towards the surface. On the other hand, if convection begins within a layer of stratus cloud, it may break up into individual cloudlets and become a layer of stratocumulus.

SPECIES OF STRATUS CLOUD
There are just two species (see page 57) of stratus cloud:
- Stratus fractus (St fra)
- Stratus nebulosus (St neb)

↑ Stratus fractus. *(Author)*

↓ Featureless stratus nebulosus, thin enough to allow the position of the Sun to be seen. *(Author)*

Mistaken identity

Stratus may sometimes be confused with other clouds, most frequently with stratocumulus, when the latter is too far away for the characteristic breaks to be obvious.

Stratus can also be confused with nimbostratus, however, both the amount of precipitation and the transparency help to distinguish between the two types. Stratus gives little or no precipitation, and this is in the form of light drizzle if it does occur. In addition, stratus is often thin enough for the outline of the Sun or Moon to be seen through it. Nimbostratus, by contrast, is very thick and produces long periods of rain, often very heavy. Nimbostratus is also usually preceded by other cloud types, notably cirrostratus and altostratus. Altostratus itself might occasionally be mistaken for stratus, but altostratus is usually noticeably higher.

Stratus fractus (St fra) (broken stratus) is often difficult to differentiate from similarly broken cumulus fractus. Generally, however, it is easy enough to tell the difference, because the two species form under different conditions. Cumulus fractus form when there are clear skies that lead to heating of the ground early in the day. They are also seen when cumulus clouds decay in the evening when heating from the Sun dies away. Stratus, by contrast, usually arises when warm air is carried over a cold surface, whether that is the land or sea (heating by the Sun is largely absent).

Stratus nebulosus (St neb) is essentially featureless and merely a sheet of even cloud. It may arise when fragments of stratus fractus gradually increase in size and merge into a single, featureless sheet.

VARIETIES OF STRATUS CLOUD
There are three varieties (see Chapter 58) of stratus cloud:
- Stratus opacus (Sc op)
- Stratus translucidus (Sc tr)
- Stratus undulatus (Sc un)

Stratus opacus (Sc op) as the name implies, is dense and does not allow the Sun or Moon to be seen through it.

↑ Stratus undulatus with unusual striated appearance. *(Duncan Waldron)*

↓ Heavy stratocumulus over Paris. *(Author)*

Stratus translucidus (Sc tr) is, by contrast, thin, and allows the outline of the Sun or Moon to be seen. Because stratus is generally a water-droplet cloud, where the droplets are all of a similar size, the sunlight or moonlight may create a coronal display (see page 102) in the thin cloud.

Stratus undulatus (Sc un) is a rare variety of stratus that displays distinct undulations on its lower surface. It is most common for these to appear downwind of some obstacle, such as a hill, that sets the air into a wave-like motion. Such waves are usually approximately at a right-angle to the direction of the wind.

Stratocumulus (Sc)

Stratocumulus shows far more variation and interest than stratus. It is the most common cloud type all over the world, and is frequently present over the oceans.

THE EVOLUTION OF STRATOCUMULUS CLOUDS

Stratocumulus (Sc) cloud may evolve from:
- Stratus (St)
- Cumulus (Cu)

Stratocumulus may form in two main ways, which are, in fact, mechanisms that are more-or-less opposite to one another. Shallow convection may set in within a layer

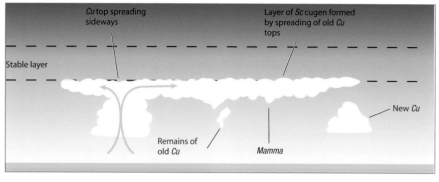

Cu top spreading sideways

Layer of Sc cugen formed by spreading of old Cu tops

Stable layer

New Cu

Remains of old Cu

Mamma

⬆ The formation of stratocumulus (or altocumulus) cumulogenitus when rising cumulus clouds encounter a stable layer. The layer tends to erode by mixing at its lower surface, sometimes producing distinct bulges or mamma. *(Ian Moores)*

⬅ A layer of stratocumulus forming from cumulus, with a separate layer of low altocumulus above. *(Author)*

Stratocumulus sky effects

Stratocumulus generally produces very little precipitation at the surface, but may show distinct fallstreaks (virga) beneath the cloud. These arise where rain is falling from the cloud, but is evaporating in the drier air beneath. Very occasionally, the base of stratocumulus may display distinct pouches (mamma, see page 87).

Because stratocumulus cloud is a water-droplet cloud, thin areas may produce a corona around the Sun or the Moon, or the edges of the patches of cloud may show iridescence. It has been known for stratocumulus clouds to show halo phenomena (see page 104) under extremely cold conditions, but this is exceptionally rare at temperate latitudes.

of stratus, which leads to the layer of cloud tending to lose heat from its upper surface, creating convection that erodes the cloud and may then break it into individual cloudlets. The other mechanism is where moderate convection from the ground creates a layer of shallow cumulus clouds, or produces thermals that rise until they encounter an inversion. The increase in temperature, combined with the air having reached its dewpoint (at which condensation occurs), causes the cloud to spread out sideways, beneath the inversion, giving rise to a layer of stratocumulus.

Stratocumulus (Sc) clouds may evolve into:

- Cumulus congestus (Cu con)
- Cumulonimbus (Cb)
- Cumulus (Cu)
- Stratus (St)

If the convection from the surface

The height of confusion

High stratocumulus may be confused with altocumulus, but there is a technical way of determining which is which. Stratocumulus elements must exceed 5° across, when measured 30° above the horizon. (Measuring angles in the sky is discussed in Chapter 6.)

becomes stronger later in the day, the thermals may break through the inversion and go on to create cumulus congestus or even cumulonimbus clouds. Such major convective clouds may be difficult to recognise from the ground, as they may be hidden by the general layer of stratocumulus, but are readily visible from aircraft flying above the layer.

Stratocumulus may decay if very strong convection develops, or if the wind speed and turbulence increase. The layer will break up, eventually becoming individual, isolated cumulus clouds. If, on the other hand, the wind drops and convection weakens – such as towards evening when the heat from the Sun declines – stratocumulus may thicken and eventually turn into a more-or-less unbroken layer of stratus.

SPECIES OF STRATOCUMULUS CLOUD

There are three species of stratocumulus:
- Stratocumulus castellanus (Sc cas)
- Stratocumulus lenticularis (Sc len)
- Stratocumulus stratiformis (Sc str)

⬇ Towers rising from a layer of stratocumulus castellanus. *(Author)*

Stratocumulus castellanus (Sc cas)

form where the top of a layer of stratocumulus develops 'turrets', where strong convection is causing the upward growth of cloud. This is normally a sign of the imminent break-up of the stratocumulus layer and even greater growth of individual cumulus congestus clouds. The castellanus species is described in more detail later (see page XX), because it can be a sign of forthcoming severe weather.

Stratocumulus lenticularis (Sc len) is

the occasional result of humid air set into waves when passing over high ground. This may produce cloud in the tops of the waves that occur downwind of the obstacle. Sometimes this form of cloud extends downwind behind a peak, forming what is known as a 'banner cloud'.

Stratocumulus stratiformis (Sc str)

often forms a more-or-less continuous sheet, right across the sky, and is particularly common over large areas of the oceans.

VARIETIES OF STRATOCUMULUS CLOUD

There are seven varieties (see Chapter 3) of stratocumulus cloud:

- Stratocumulus duplicatus (Sc du)
- Stratocumulus lacunosus (Sc la)
- Stratocumulus opacus (Sc op)
- Stratocumulus perlucidus (Sc pe)
- Stratocumulus radiatus (Sc ra)
- Stratocumulus translucidus (Sc tr)
- Stratocumulus undulates (Sc un)

Stratocumulus duplicatus (Sc du)

forms in two distinct layers at different altitudes. This is difficult to see from the ground, because the lower layer tends to block any view of the higher clouds. It is easier to see from high ground or an aircraft, if the observer is above the lower layer of cloud.

Stratocumulus lacunosus (Sc la) is a

rare form of stratocumulus where the cloud

masses are not in the form of individual patches, but instead form a network of cloud, rather like a net, with large 'holes', showing clear sky.

Stratocumulus opacus (Sc op) is a variety where, as the name implies, although the Sun and Moon may be glimpsed in the gaps between the individual cloud masses, they are completely hidden when behind the actual patches of cloud.

Stratocumulus perlucidus (Sc pe) is the most common variety of stratocumulus, and takes the form of individual flat 'pancakes' of cloud. The layer has substantial gaps, through which blue sky is visible (or the Sun and Moon). The patches of cloud not only appear larger in extent than the corresponding individual cloudlets in the higher altocumulus and cirrocumulus, but, individually, they do actually cover a larger area.

Stratocumulus radiatus (Sc ra) occurs in long rows, with just narrow gaps between the individual cloud elements. This species is much rarer than the somewhat similar cumulus form: cumulus radiatus (Cu ra), described earlier.

Stratocumulus translucidus (Sc tr) comprises thin individual cloud elements, which allow the outline of the Sun or Moon to be seen through them.

Stratocumulus undulatus (Sc un) occurs in billows, where there are distinct, separate rolls of cloud. These generally lie at right-angles to the wind direction, and tend to arise when there is a fairly strong vertical wind shear – a difference in wind strength or direction at different heights – which creates a vertical rolling circulation within the individual bands of cloud.

⬆ Distinct billows in a layer of stratocumulus undulatus. *(Author)*

⬇ Billows (the undulatus variety) arise in thin stratiform cloud when there is vertical wind shear between two adjacent layers. *(Ian Moores)*

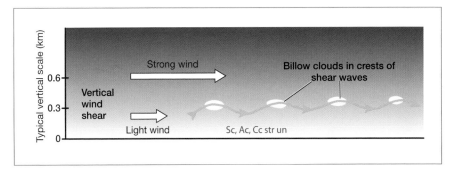

Medium-level clouds

Medium-level clouds are defined as those that generally have bases at altitudes of between 2 and 6km (approximately 6,500 and 20,000ft).

There are three genera of clouds in the middle level:

- Altostratus (As)
- Altocumulus (Ac)
- Nimbostratus (Ns)

However, the last of these – nimbostratus – is often a very deep cloud, extending down towards the surface and upwards into the highest level.

Altostratus (As)

Altostratus is often associated with depression systems, where it forms part of a sequence that is a reliable sign of an approaching system (and the bad weather that normally accompanies it).

Altostratus is basically a featureless cloud and, like nimbostratus, it does not have any distinct species, unlike all the other cloud genera. It may be extremely extensive (perhaps hundreds of kilometres across) and is generally very thick, often amounting to thousands of metres in depth. It is usually very uniform in appearance, although occasionally streaks (striations) are visible, so that it seems slightly fibrous.

Altostratus cloud may produce considerable quantities of rain or, when conditions are suitable, snow or ice pellets, and such precipitation may persist for long periods of time. The precipitation may reach the ground, but often occurs in the form of virga (see page 88) or fallstreaks, that evaporate into the air beneath the cloud. These streaks are often responsible for the cloud's streaked appearance. The evaporation of the precipitation into the layer of air beneath the altostratus causes that layer to become saturated and may then give rise to the accessory cloud known as pannus (stratus fractus). Sometimes this scattered cloud may gradually extend and thicken and even itself become a layer of more-or-less continuous cloud.

Key features of altostratus (As)

- An extensive, grey or blue-grey layer cloud, sometimes light, but often very dark.
- Normally fairly uniform in appearance, although it may appear streaked and slightly fibrous.
- Often produces large quantities of precipitation, some of which may reach the ground.

⬇ Altostratus and some lower pannus. *(Author)*

Altostratus sky effects

Altostratus is often a mixed cloud, consisting of both tiny water droplets and minute ice crystals, which may be mixed with larger raindrops and snowflakes. When the cloud is thin, it may be possible to see the Sun or Moon through it, but because it is a mixed cloud, it does not display any halo phenomena (see page 104). Under these circumstances, it has a highly characteristic appearance, because the bodies appear as if seen through ground glass. When it is thicker, however, especially as it thickens ahead of an approaching depression system, the Sun will be completely hidden, and not even its position may be readily determined. The light that penetrates altostratus is diffuse, being scattered by all the particles within the cloud, and objects on the ground fail to cast any shadows, because the light arrives from a whole range of directions.

Sometimes the edges of a sheet of altostratus – especially if the cloud is decaying – may contain just water droplets. These areas often display colourful iridescence (see page 102) or even a corona (or part of one) around the Sun or Moon.

⬇ Steadily thickening altostratus ahead of an approaching warm front. *(Author)*

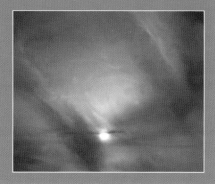

The base of an altostratus layer may sometimes develop mamma (pouches), which are the signs of descending currents of cold air beneath the cloud.

THE EVOLUTION OF ALTOSTRATUS CLOUDS

Altostratus (As) clouds may evolve from:
- Cirrostratus (Cs)
- Nimbostratus (Ns)
- Cumulonimbus (Cb)

As with other stratiform clouds, the most frequent way in which altostratus is formed is by the slow uplift of a humid layer of air. This most commonly occurs ahead of an advancing depression system, when warm, moist air gradually ascends at the warm front. The altostratus often develops from the higher cirrostratus cloud, which gradually thickens and lowers, but may sometimes be preceded by scattered patches of altocumulus. The reverse process may occur when, as a depression passes away, the thick, rain-bearing nimbostratus cloud gradually thins and becomes a sheet of altostratus.

Occasionally, especially in the tropics, large cumulonimbus clouds or major thunderstorm systems may spread out at an intermediate level and produce altostratus cloud. Although small fragments of altostratus may occur ahead of such systems, generally the cloud trails behind the active storm system. This type of formation of altostratus is uncommon at higher latitudes (in the temperate zones), where such active systems tend to produce stratus or stratocumulus clouds, rather than the higher altostratus.

Altostratus (As) clouds may evolve into:
- Nimbostratus (Ns)
- Altocumulus (Ac)

Frequently, an altostratus layer thickens considerably and turns into a layer of thick nimbostratus, which will give heavy rain at the surface.

Like the other stratiform clouds (stratus and cirrostratus), convection may occur within a layer of altostratus, and break up the layer into individual cloud masses. It then becomes altocumulus. To be classed as such, the individual 'pancakes' of cloud must be between 1 and 5° across, measured 30° from the horizon. (As mentioned in the 'Height of confusion' box on page 61, stratocumulus elements always exceed 5° in size –

⬇ Altostratus duplicatus with some altocumulus. (*Author*)

measuring angles in the sky is discussed in Chapter 6.)

SPECIES AND VARIETIES OF ALTOSTRATUS CLOUD

Although altostratus displays no distinct species, there are five varieties:
- Altostratus duplicatus (As du)
- Altostratus opacus (As op)
- Altostratus radiatus (As ra)
- Altostratus translucidus (As tr)
- Altostratus undulatus (As un)

Altostratus duplicatus (As du) exists in two or more layers, although this is often difficult to see. The layers are sometimes visible at the edge of altostratus sheets that have been formed from the spreading out of altocumulus, rather than the encroachment of a major sheet of altostratus ahead of a depression.

Altostratus opacus (As op) is so dense that in completely hides the Sun or Moon.

Altostratus radiatus (As ra) is a form of altostratus which has become organised into parallel lines extending downwind, but unlike cumulus radiatus, the condition is rarely seen.

Altostratus translucidus (As tr) is thin enough for the position of the Sun (or occasionally, the Moon) to be determined through it, although with a diffuse outline.

Altostratus undulatus (As un) has parallel undulations, at right-angles to the wind direction. This may arise because the air has been set into wave motion by the wind blowing over hills or mountains,

↑ Altostratus undulatus over New South Wales. *(Duncan Waldron)*

↑ A sheet of altocumulus. *(Author)*

or because there is vertical wind shear, with the wind strength increasing rapidly with an increase in height.

Altocumulus (Ac)

Altocumulus produces some of the most striking and varied skies. This arises because there are four distinct species and no fewer than seven varieties, and also because, being a broken cloud that occurs at medium altitudes, it is often easy to see, and undergoes dramatic changes in its appearance with the changing illumination at sunrise and sunset.

In many of its features altocumulus resembles the lower stratocumulus and the higher cirrocumulus. It occurs as a similar type of rounded masses of cloud, with clear sky between them. It is distinguished from those two cloud genera by the size of the individual elements. A cloud is classed as altocumulus if, 30° or more above the horizon, the average size of an individual cloud element lies between 5° and 1°. Larger elements indicate stratocumulus, or smaller cirrocumulus. Another distinguishing feature is the strength of the shading, which is distinct, but not

extremely dark, again falling somewhere between the stratocumulus (which has dark shading) and cirrocumulus (which shows no shading at all).

In general, altocumulus occurs as an extensive sheet of cloud, consisting of more or less regular smaller cloud elements. As with stratocumulus and cirrocumulus, these may be in the form of small rounded clumps; larger, flatter 'pancakes'; or extensive rolls of cloud. Blue sky is usually clearly visible between the individual elements. Various

Key features of altocumulus (Ac)

- A white to pale grey cloud that generally occurs in a distinct layer as heaps, rolls or pancakes, with darker shading.
- Blue sky is usually clearly visible between the individual elements.
- It sometimes gives rise to precipitation, but only rarely does this reach the ground.

other forms also occur. These may take the form of smooth, lens-shaped clouds (lenticular clouds); tufts with ragged bases (often with distinct virga or fallstreaks); and cloud turrets that rise from a common base (all these are described in more detail later under the various species). The height of altocumulus enables us to see many more of the individual cloud elements than with the lower stratocumulus, so the sky often appears full of innumerable masses of cloud.

THE EVOLUTION OF ALTOCUMULUS CLOUDS

Altocumulus (Ac) clouds may evolve from:
- Altostratus (As)
- Nimbostratus (Ns)
- Stratocumulus Sc)
- Cumulus (Cu)

As with stratocumulus (and also cirrocumulus), altocumulus forms either through the break-up of existing cloud, particularly altostratus, or through the uplift of a humid layer of air. Once again, if a sheet of unbroken cloud loses heat from its upper surface to space, it tends to break up into individual convection cells. The cloud thickens in the centre of each cell, and dissipates around the edges, giving rise to a sheet of altocumulus. Broken altocumulus elements are often found around the fringes of a more extensive sheet of altostratus. The sizes of the individual cells are less than those found in stratocumulus, and the overall thickness of the cloud is generally much less.

A decaying sheet of nimbostratus may sometimes leave altocumulus clouds behind it. This frequently occurs with the passage of fronts in a depression system. Sometimes deep stratocumulus may break up with the higher levels turning into

Altocumulus sky effects

The transparency of altocumulus varies considerably. On occasions, individual elements may be dense enough to completely mask the Sun and Moon, but on others they are thin enough for the positions to be determined quite easily. Altocumulus often consists solely of fine water droplets (frequently in the supercooled state) but, at lower temperatures, it may also be a mixed cloud that contains ice crystals. As a result, altocumulus clouds may display optical phenomena associated either with water droplets (such as coronae or iridescence) or with ice crystals (such as haloes, parhelia and sun pillars). When the individual elements are close together, the base of thick altocumulus often displays a lumpy appearance, which may become extremely marked when illuminated at a shallow angle by the rays of the rising or setting Sun.

altocumulus. This type of cloud may also occur through the thickening of individual patches of cirrostratus, especially ahead of an advancing warm front.

In a similar fashion to the way that cumulus clouds may spread out to produce a layer of stratocumulus, so they may also reach a stable layer at a higher level and expand sideway to create a sheet of altocumulus. Altocumulus is also frequently seen ahead of major thunderstorm systems, and often trails behind them.

SPECIES OF ALTOCUMULUS CLOUD

There are four, very distinctive species of altocumulus:

↑ Altocumulus castellanus in lines. *(Author)*

↑ Altocumulus floccus. *(Author)*

■ Altocumulus castellanus (Ac cas)
▩ Altocumulus floccus (Ac flo)
■ Altocumulus lenticularis (Ac len)
▩ Altocumulus stratiformis (Ac str)

Altocumulus castellanus (Ac cas) has distinct cloud towers or turrets that rise from the otherwise fairly uniform layer of cloud, and are a sign of instability at that level. The cloud turrets often arise from an individual line of cloud. This upward growth is one of the indicators that vigorous convection may occur within the near future, and that there is the chance of strong thunderstorm activity.

Altocumulus floccus (Ac flo) consists of small individual, more-or-less rounded tufts of cloud, which may display ragged bases

or trailing fallstreaks (virga). They often appear in considerable numbers, giving the sky an extremely striking appearance. Although normally quite widely separated, they sometimes occur in more closely packed lines. They are another sure sign of instability and often an indication of thundery activity to come.

Altocumulus lenticularis (Ac len) are usually highly distinctive. They are smooth lens- or almond-shaped clouds that hang stationary in the sky, often for extended

⬇ Humid layers of air will give rise to a succession of lenticular clouds in the crests of lee waves. Under certain circumstances, a lee rotor may form, with the surface wind blowing towards the high ground. *(Ian Moores)*

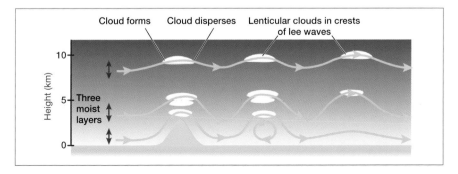

← Altocumulus lenticularis on two different levels, generated by a wind from the left. Lower cumulus clouds are visible, together with the suggestion of a second wave-crest at the higher level. *(Author)*

periods. They arise in the crests of waves that are produced when a stable layer of air is forced to rise over hills or mountain peaks. Their smooth outlines are particularly striking, as is the fact that they seem

Pile of plates

Sometimes multiple humid layers may produce lenticular clouds one above the other, and this striking appearance is known as a 'pile d'assiettes' (French for 'pile of plates').

→ Multiple layers of lenticular (wave) clouds above Boambee, New South Wales. *(Duncan Waldron)*

⬇ A drawing of 'a remarkable cloud' over Madeira by Charles Piazzi Smyth.

⬇ A 'pile d'assiettes' over Madeira.

→ Well-developed wave clouds (altocumulus lenticularis) above the mountains of Norway, photographed from a meteorological research aircraft. *(Wood)*

unchanging, hanging in the sky for hours on end. However, if they are examined in detail – with binoculars, for example – it is usually possible to see slight fluctuations where they are forming at the leading edge and dissipating on the downwind (trailing) side. Under certain conditions, individual clouds may merge to form greatly elongated, smooth lines of cloud. Altocumulus lenticularis, like other wave clouds, tend to persist while the wind speed and direction remain constant.

Altocumulus stratiformis (Ac str) is an extensive sheet of cloud, rather than just small patches. The fact that essentially all of the visible sky is covered by a regular pattern of cloudlets in a conspicuous layer often leads to a very striking appearance, often called a 'mackerel sky', although this term is also applied to the higher cirrocumulus. As the light changes, this effect can disappear.

VARIETIES OF ALTOCUMULUS CLOUD
Altocumulus displays a wide range of varieties, of which there are seven distinct forms:
- Altocumulus duplicatus (Ac du)
- Altocumulus lacunosus (Ac la)
- Altocumulus opacus (Ac op)
- Altocumulus perlucidus (Ac pe)
- Altocumulus radiatus (Ac ra)
- Altocumulus translucidus (Ac tr)
- Altocumulus undulatus (Ac un)

Altocumulus duplicatus (Ac du) comprises multiple layers of cloud. Because of its height, it is normally somewhat easier to see the layered effect than with the lower stratocumulus.

Altocumulus lacunosus (Ac la) is a reversal of the normal appearance of a sheet of individual cloud elements, and is a network of cloud with large clear holes. This variety is relatively rare.

↓ Altocumulus lacunosus. *(Author)*

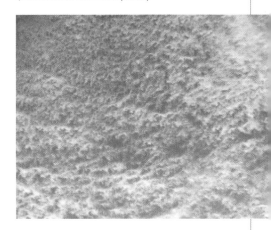

Altocumulus opacus (Ac op) is an extensive sheet of altocumulus which is dense enough to hide the Sun or Moon.

Altocumulus perlucidus (Ac pe) is a sheet of altocumulus with clear gaps between the elements, through which blue sky is clearly visible. This is probably the most common variety of altocumulus, and it often arises when shallow convection begins within an otherwise unbroken sheet of altostratus cloud.

Altocumulus radiatus (Ac ra) is a form of altocumulus where the individual elements are arranged in parallel lines. In this form, the clouds often grow upward to form the species altocumulus castellanus.

Altocumulus translucidus (Ac tr) comprises thin individual cloud elements, which allows the position of the Sun or Moon to be seen through them. This variety is perhaps more common than the opacus variety just described.

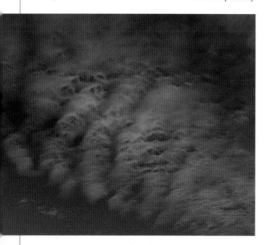

⬇ Distinct billows in altocumulus undulatus. *(Author)*

Altocumulus undulatus (Ac un) is a form of altocumulus that has developed a series of undulations, which may be distinct rolls of cloud, forming billows. The undulations are at right-angles to the wind at cloud level.

Nimbostratus (Ns)

The final genus of middle-level clouds is nimbostratus. Unfortunately, it is also the more boring of all cloud genera! Nimbostratus clouds are very familiar. They are the clouds that bring the heavy and seemingly endless rain or snow that accompanies the depressions that march across the UK.

Nimbostratus is classified as a middle-level cloud, but often has a very low base, sometimes reaching down to just above the ground and may touch the tops of hills or mountains, which it will drench with rain. Although it is not apparent from the surface, the cloud is often extremely deep, extending high into the atmosphere, well above the height of 6km (about 20,000ft) at which cloud genera are regarded as belonging to the 'high' level.

Nimbostratus has no recognised species, nor varieties. It is always grey, or dark grey, and gives rise to heavy precipitation in the form of rain or snow. This precipitation is generally more-or-less continuous, although it is often organised into bands, where there are 'pulses' of heavier rain or snow, followed by short spells when there seems to be a temporary respite from the relentless downpour. The precipitation is usually widespread and may last for a very long time: hours or even days.

The composition of nimbostratus varies greatly, and largely depends on temperature. It may sometimes consist entirely of water droplets of various sizes (that is, both tiny cloud droplets and larger raindrops) and at other times is may consist of ice crystals and large snowflakes. It may sometimes be a mixed cloud, like altostratus, when both water droplets and ice crystals are present at the same level.

The cloud is always so dense that it completely hides the Sun or Moon, and because of its density, it never produces any optical effects. Because is it always the source of precipitation, its base appears soft, diffuse, or ragged. This base is often partly hidden by ragged pannus (generally stratus fractus, but occasionally looking like cumulus fractus) that has formed in the saturated air beneath the main cloud layer.

On slow-moving occluded fronts (see page 26), nimbostratus sometimes produces days of fairly continuous rain or snow and is often the cause of widespread flooding or record-breaking snowfalls.

↑ Rain-bearing nimbostratus. *(Author)*

THE EVOLUTION OF NIMBOSTRATUS CLOUDS
Nimbostratus may evolve from:
- Altostratus (As)
- Altocumulus (Ac)
- Stratocumulus (Sc)
- Cumulonimbus (Cb)
- Cumulus congestus (Cu con)

The most widespread layers of nimbostratus arise as a result of the slow uplift of moist air in a depression, generally at the advancing warm front. Here, it is very frequently preceded by altostratus, which thickens and lowers towards the surface, almost imperceptibly turning into nimbostratus.

Nimbostratus may very occasionally result from the thickening of a layer of altocumulus or stratocumulus. Large cumulonimbus clouds or thunderstorm systems may sometimes spread out and give rise to a layer of nimbostratus, but this always covers a much smaller area than the extensive sheets that are created by depressions. On very rare occasions, nimbostratus may also arise from large, rain-bearing cumulus congestus clouds. Once again, the horizontal extent of any resulting sheet of cloud is small.

Key features of nimbostratus (Ns)

- A heavy, thick, grey or dark grey cloud with a soft, diffuse or ragged base.
- Always completely masks the Sun of Moon.
- Forms extremely widespread sheets, often with a very low base.
- Gives rise to heavy, prolonged precipitation, sometimes lasting for many hours, or even days.

High-level clouds

High-level clouds are defined as those that have bases at, or above an altitude of 6km (approximately 20,000ft).

There are three genera of high clouds:
- Cirrus (Ci)
- Cirrostratus (Cs)
- Cirrocumulus (Cc)

⬆ High-level cirrus clouds, showing considerable wind shear aloft, ahead of a warm front approaching from the west (left). *(Author)*

Cirrus (Ci)

Cirrus clouds are wispy clouds consisting of ice crystals that occur high in the atmosphere. They are very familiar, especially the form known popularly as 'mare's tails'. They are the highest of the main cloud genera, and may sometimes even occur in the lower stratosphere.

Cirrus clouds occur as fine trails or filaments of cloud, and may sometimes have a silken appearance. Depending on circumstances, they may be relatively straight, curved, hooked, or occasionally they seem randomly entangled. Frequently cirrus takes the form of a hooked shape, at the top of which there is a small wispy tuft of cloud, known as the generating head.

Cirrus often appears in parallel bands that apparently radiate from one point of

⬇ Jet-stream cirrus streaming north over Edinburgh. *(Author)*

⬇ The northern Polar Front jet stream over Nova Scotia, flowing eastwards above the Atlantic, photographed from orbit. *(NASA)*

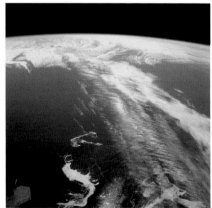

the sky. This type of structure is frequently seen in jet streams. Indeed jet streams, normally unseen, are made visible by the cirrus carried along by the high-speed, high-altitude winds. Cirrus billows are also commonly observed in jet streams.

Frequently, cirrus appears as small tufts with trailing wisps of ice crystals (virga). Sometimes such tufts of cloud may form in otherwise clear air.

Generally, cirrus is so high in the sky that it appears white, and often brighter than any other clouds in the sky. When particularly dense it may seem grey in colour, especially when seen against the light. Because it is so high it goes through a whole sequence of colours at sunset (and a corresponding reversed sequence at sunrise, of course.) At sunset it remains white when the lower clouds have changed colour. When the Sun has set below the horizon, the lower clouds have become dark and appear as dark silhouettes against the brilliantly coloured high clouds.

THE EVOLUTION OF CIRRUS CLOUDS
Cirrus (Ci) clouds may evolve from:
- Cirrocumulus (Cc)
- Altocumulus (Ac)
- Cirrostratus (Cs)
- Cumulonimbus (Cb)
- Aircraft contrails

Although cirrus often forms in a clear sky, it may also arise from the virga (fallstreaks) that frequently occur with cirrocumulus and altocumulus, or else through the decay of the thinner portions of a sheet of cirrostratus. An additional source is the cirrus plumes that are often produced by giant cumulonimbus clouds. Such plumes often persist long after the parent clouds have dissipated.

Key features of cirrus (Ci)

- Consists of fibrous streaks of ice crystals.
- Generally appears white, but may seem grey when particularly dense and also when seen against the light.
- Does not give any precipitation at the ground, but may often display optical phenomena.

Cirrus sky effects

Cirrus clouds often exhibit optical phenomena, such as parhelia ('mock suns' – see page 105), which are frequently brilliantly coloured and much brighter than those that appear in cirrostratus cloud.

Cirrus also often forms from the contrails (condensation trails) of aircraft. Under certain conditions, contrails do not dissipate but may persist for hours, spreading into broad bands of cirrus that may cover a large portion of the sky.

SPECIES OF CIRRUS CLOUD
There are five distinct species of cirrus:
- Cirrus castellanus (Ci cas)
- Cirrus fibratus (Ci fib)
- Cirrus floccus (Ci flo)
- Cirrus uncinus (Ci unc)
- Cirrus spissatus (Ci spi)

Cirrus castellanus (Ci cas) are tufts of cirrus cloud showing distinct signs of beginning upward growth. This cirrus castellanus species is relatively

⬆ Well-developed cirrus uncinus. *(Author)*

⬆ Cirrus vertebratus. *(Author)*

uncommon, because it indicates that there is instability at that great height, which may allow the clouds to expand upwards.

Cirrus fibratus (Ci fib) exists as long, relatively straight or slightly curved, fibrous streamers. These do not appear to originate in the tufts of cloud that are the generating heads, nor do they show distinct hooks.

Cirrus floccus (Ci flo) consists of small puffs of cloud, usually with ragged bases, and these sometimes stream away as fallstreaks (virga).

Cirrus spissatus (Ci spi) is dense cirrus that will partially or completely hide the Sun (or Moon). It appears dark grey when it is seen against the light. Extremely dense cirrus spissatus plumes sometimes form at the top of active cumulonimbus clouds.

Cirrus uncinus (Ci unc) show distinct hooks (the word *uncinus* is Latin for 'hook') These generally occur close to the generating heads of clouds, where ice crystals form, before falling out of

the cloud and producing the long trailing streamers.

VARIETIES OF CIRRUS CLOUD
There are four varieties of cirrus:
- Cirrus duplicatus (Ci du)
- Cirrus intortus (Ci in)
- Cirrus radiatus (Ci ra)
- Cirrus vertebratus (Ci ve)

Cirrus duplicatus (Ci du) is a cirrus cloud that occurs at more than one level.

Cirrus intortus (Ci in) takes the form of tangled skeins of cirrus. The streaks of ice crystals appear to be randomly entangled by upper-atmosphere winds. This variety is unique to cirrus cloud.

Cirrus radiatus (Ci ra) forms in long lines across the sky. It is particularly commonly found in jet-stream cirrus, when the streaks run parallel to the winds at height.

Cirrus vertebratus (Ci ve) resembles the ribs or vertebrae of a skeleton, or else to the bones of a fish. This variety is rare and is exclusive to cirrus.

Cirrostratus (Cs)

Cirrostratus is a high cloud that is often overlooked, yet it displays some of the most striking halo phenomena, and is also a significant early indicator of a possible deterioration in the weather.

A thin veil of this high cloud frequently steals across the sky. Only when the sunshine seems to have lost some of its heat do people realise that a change has taken place. Cirrostratus is sometimes completely smooth in appearance, and only reveals its presence when a blue sky becomes slightly milky. More frequently, however, on close examination, cirrostratus shows a fibrous structure.

The edge of a layer of cirrostratus may be quite sharp, but often it is preceded by initial, isolated wisps of cirrus. These gradually become more numerous until they form a sheet of cirrostratus partially or completely covering the sky. This type of

Cirrostratus sky effects

Probably the most striking feature of cirrostratus is that it exhibits a whole range of halo phenomena: 22° and 46° haloes, parhelia (mock suns), and various other arcs and points of light. These effects (which are described in detail later on pages 104–106) are so common that they are a good sign of the presence of cirrostratus. Once again, they are generally overlooked. The optical phenomena are most marked when the sheet of cirrostratus is thin and gradually disappear as it thickens.

⬇ A typical sheet of cirrostratus, with a 22° solar halo. *(Author)*

Key features of cirrostratus (Cs)

- A thin sheet of ice-crystal cloud, often striated, which frequently exhibits halo phenomena.
- Does not give rise to any precipitation at the ground.

change commonly occurs with the approach of the warm front in a depression system, and the cirrostratus itself gradually thickens, lowers towards the surface, and eventually turns into altostratus. Cirrostratus itself is so thin that the light from the Sun always casts shadows.

↓ An extensive sheet, rather unusually dense, of cirrostratus fibratus. *(Author)*

THE EVOLUTION OF CIRROSTRATUS CLOUDS

Cirrostratus (Cs) clouds may evolve from:
- Cirrus (Ci)
- Cirrocumulus (Cc)
- Cumulonimbus (Cb)
- Altostratus (As)

Cirrostratus generally occurs as the first sign of an approaching depression (more specifically, of an approaching warm front). It arises from the gradual ascent of warm air and the slow merger of streaks of cirrus. A sheet of cirrostratus may also arise from the ice crystals that fall from cirrocumulus clouds, or by the spreading out of the cirrus plumes at the top of cumulonimbus clouds. Less frequently it remains behind when altostratus clouds decay.

SPECIES OF CIRROSTRATUS CLOUD

There are just two species of cirrostratus:
- Cirrostratus fibratus (Cs fib)
- Cirrostratus nebulosus (Cs neb)

Cirrostratus fibratus (Cs fib) exhibits some fibrous structure. The streaks are simply trails of ice crystals that show up against the main cloud background

Cirrostratus nebulosus (Ci neb) appears as a featureless and completely uniform thin veil covering the sky. The position of the Sun is visible through it, but otherwise there are no recognisable features.

VARIETIES OF CIRROSTRATUS CLOUD
There are just two varieties of cirrostratus:
- Cirrostratus duplicatus (Cs du)
- Cirrostratus undulatus (Cs un)

Cirrostratus duplicatus (Cs du) comprises layers of cirrostratus, although these may be difficult to detect, especially with cirrostratus nebulosus. The different layers become most apparent around sunset and sunrise, when the changing illumination, and consequent alterations in colour and brightness of the layers helps to differentiate between them.

Cirrostratus undulatus (Cs un) is undulating cirrostratus, although the undulations are often difficult to detect, especially in the middle of the day, or when the cloud is directly overhead. The undulations become more apparent towards the horizon, and may become very striking around sunrise or sunset, when grazing illumination throws the crests and troughs into sharply defined relief. Under such conditions cirrostratus then bears some resemblance to the much higher and more finely structured noctilucent clouds (see page 92) that are occasionally visible in the middle of summer nights.

Cirrocumulus (Cc)
As with cirrostratus, the last of the high clouds, cirrocumulus, is often inconspicuous and overlooked. This is both because it may be very thin, and also because the individual cloud elements are small. A cloud is defined as cirrocumulus if the individual elements are less than one 1° across, measured 30° above the horizon.

Cirrocumulus is white or pale blue and occurs in patches or larger layers, which consists of small elements that are rounded masses and ripples, which may be separate or partially merged. Unlike stratocumulus or altocumulus elements, the individual cloudlets never show any shading. Cirrocumulus is generally far less

The even size of the cloud particles may produce optical phenomena in the form of coronae (see page 102) around the Sun or Moon and iridescence (see page 102), which is usually visible along the edges of the cloud.

distinctive than the similar lower clouds, altocumulus and stratocumulus. This is not only because, being higher, the individual cloud elements appear smaller, but also because it is much thinner than the lower genera. Among these three cloud types there is a direct relationship between the height of the cloud and the thickness of the layer and the individual elements: the lower the cloud, the thicker the cloud. Cirrocumulus is frequently so thin that it appears merely as delicate ripples of cloud. These are often so low in contrast that they are difficult to distinguish from the blue sky above them.

The cloud mainly consists of ice crystals, which exist alongside some supercooled water droplets, although the latter tend to be converted into ice very rapidly. Being so thin and transparent, cirrocumulus always allows the position of the Sun and Moon to be detected, and objects on the ground always cast shadows, unlike the situation with altostratus.

THE EVOLUTION OF CIRROCUMULUS CLOUDS
Cirrocumulus may evolve from:
- Cirrostratus (Cs)
- Altocumulus (Ac)

Cirrocumulus may arise from a layer of cirrostratus, in which shallow convection begins to occur, breaking up the layer into individual cloud elements. Similarly, the decay of a sheet of altocumulus may sometimes leave behind a patch of cirrocumulus. Unlike the other high clouds, cirrus and cirrostratus, cirrocumulus is always broken up into tiny cloudlets and ripples. Most of any cirrocumulus sheet consists of these small rounded cloud masses, although it may also contain some parts that appear fibrous or smooth.

SPECIES OF CIRROCUMULUS CLOUD
There are four species of cirrocumulus:
- Cirrocumulus castellanus (Cc cas)
- Cirrocumulus floccus (Cc flo)
- Cirrocumulus lenticularis (Cc len)
- Cirrocumulus stratiformis (Cc str)

Cirrocumulus castellanus (Cc cas) exhibits turrets or columns of cloud that rise from a lower base, which is often in the form of a line of cloud. The towers are often difficult to see when the cloud is more-or-less immediately overhead, but are easier to see in the distance. This variety is an indication that the air is unstable at height, and may encourage the upward growth of clouds such as cumulonimbus.

Cirrocumulus floccus (Cc flo) consists of small tufts of cloud, generally with rounded heads and more ragged bases, which sometimes have distinct fallstreaks (virga). This cloud is often present in great numbers, forming a layer right across the sky, and is an indication of instability at that level.

Cirrocumulus lenticularis (Cc len) is another form of wave cloud, and may sometimes appear in isolation, high above the mountains that are creating the wave. They are also commonly seen along with altocumulus lenticularis, when they indicate the existence of multiple humid layers in the atmosphere. This cloud is often extremely thin, but because it consists of evenly sized particles, it may show significant iridescence (see page 102).

Cirrocumulus stratiformis (Cc str) represents an extensive sheet of tiny cirrocumulus cloudlets. This may cover a substantial portion of the sky. Although always thin, when light from the rising or setting Sun shines directly along the layer, it may show signs of shading, which is absent at other times.

VARIETIES OF CIRROCUMULUS CLOUD
There are two varieties of cirrocumulus that may sometimes be encountered:
- Cirrocumulus undulatus (Cc un)
- Cirrocumulus lacunosus (Cc la)

Cirrocumulus undulatus (Cc un) comprises individual small heaps of cloud that may be arranged in rows, which have clear gaps between them. The individual cloudlets may be approximately circular, and may themselves be elongated parallel to the length of the rows, or else be billows that lie at right-angles to the prevailing wind at that height.

Cirrocumulus lacunosus (Cc la) is relatively rare, and consists of a layer of cloud with approximately circular holes, giving a net-like appearance. It generally occurs over only a small area of sky, rather than an extensive layer, but small patches occur quite frequently, surrounded by other cirriform cloud.

↑ A sheet of cirrocumulus stratiformis, grading into a thicker sheet of Cirrostratus in the distance. *(Author)*

↓ Part of a very extensive sheet of cirrocumulus lacunosus. *(Author)*

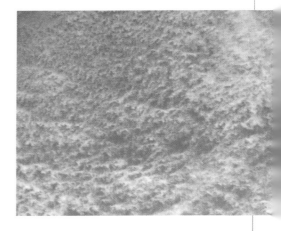

Cumulonimbus (cb)

The final cloud genus is that of cumulonimbus clouds. They are the giants among clouds. They are sometimes described with the low-level clouds, because their bases are often below 2km (approximately 6,500ft).

Their bases may be close to the ground, but their tops tower right up into the atmosphere. They often reach right though the troposphere (the lowest layer of the atmosphere), in which most weather occurs, and may reach the tropopause. At that level they encounter an inversion, where the temperature begins to rise, so their upward growth is arrested. Even when relatively small, they may bring heavy downpours of rain, while larger systems give rise to thunder and lightning, hail, violent winds, and even, in the largest systems, destructive tornadoes.

These clouds are large, towering high into the sky and extending over wide areas of countryside. Frequently they cover such a large area that the clouds' characteristic features are difficult to see unless one is at a considerable distance and has a clear view. They are always extremely dense clouds that appear brilliantly white when fully illuminated by the Sun. By contrast, they may seem exceptionally dark grey or even black when viewed against the sunlight. Cumulonimbus bases are always extremely dark and ragged, with falling rain, hail or, under certain conditions, snow. This precipitation is often in the form of fallstreaks (virga).

Once the top of the cloud becomes fibrous, it may also spread out into another highly characteristic form, that of a flattened anvil (cumulonimbus incus), or appear as a plume of cirrus, which may be rapidly drawn out across the sky by high-altitude winds. This form is particularly common if the rising cloud reaches the tropopause, where the inversion prevents further ascent. If the cloud is particularly vigorous, its impetus may carry it a short way into the stratosphere, where it

Cumulonimbus weather warning

The growth of a cumulonimbus is a warning of potentially severe weather, and so it is important to identify it correctly, particularly the way in which a deep cumulus congestus cloud becomes a true cumulonimbus. Not only do these clouds give heavy precipitation, including damaging hail, but they may also produce violent gusts and changes of wind direction, as well as lightning and other hazards. Cumulonimbus may build up into massive walls of cloud or more complex and violent systems, known as squall lines, and multicell or supercell storms. The last of these may spawn highly destructive tornadoes.

Sometimes cumulonimbus clouds may be relatively small and of limited horizontal extent. They may consist of just a single active cell, but frequently several cells in various stages of growth may be clustered together in a single system. Both types are generally described by meteorologists and weather forecasters as 'showers'.

forms a heap of cloud, known as an overshooting top (shown in a satellite view on page 30). Such overshooting tops are difficult to see from ground level, but are often visible from aircraft.

THE EVOLUTION OF CUMULONIMBUS CLOUDS

Cumulonimbus evolves from:
■ Cumulus congestus (Cu con)

Cumulonimbus clouds frequently tower through all three of the levels by which clouds are classified (low, medium and high). When growing, their tops often consist of multiple, rounded, rising heads of cloud, which are cells driven by rising thermals. Normally some of these cells – the lower ones, or those that are growing particularly rapidly – appear hard and sharp against the sky. Some of the highest cloud towers lose their hard outline and show a slightly softer appearance, which generally soon becomes fibrous. These features, together with the presence of

Anvil clouds

The highly characteristic 'anvil' shape that occurs only with cumulonimbus clouds is known as the cumulonimbus incus species. Anvils develop when the cloud reaches a major inversion, often at the tropopause. The ice crystals at the top of the cloud are carried sideways, producing the flattened cirrus shield. Generally, with strong convection, the cloud does expand slightly upwind, but most of the crystals are carried downwind, leading to the classic anvil shape. Mamma (see page 87) often develop beneath the overhanging anvil.

↓A well-developed cumulonimbus incus (anvil) cloud that has expanded at the tropopause, with an older anvil partially visible in the distance. *(Claudia Hinz)*

Key features of cumulonimbus (Cb)

- A giant, deep cloud, with a dark base and brilliantly white top when fully illuminated by sunlight; or exceptionally dark grey or black against sunlight.
- Top may be rounded but starting to lose its hard appearance, or may have become ragged in the form of a cirrus plume, or flat anvil.
- May produce heavy precipitation, as well as lightning and thunder.

precipitation beneath the cloud, positively identify the cloud as a cumulonimbus, rather than a cumulus congestus. They mark this type of cloud's two species: cumulonimbus calvus and cumulonimbus capillatus, described in more detail shortly.

Cumulonimbus may evolve into:
- Cirrus (Ci)

As mentioned previously, once the top of a cumulonimbus cloud becomes fibrous, it may also appear as a plume of cirrus, which may be rapidly drawn out across the sky by high-altitude winds.

SPECIES OF CUMULONIMBUS CLOUD

There are just two cumulonimbus species and these are unique to the genus:
- Cumulonimbus calvus (Cb cal)
- Cumulonimbus capillatus (Cb cap)

Cumulonimbus calvus (Cb cal) is the first stage in the transition to a true cumulonimbus. The tops of any rising cells lose their hard outline and become softer. (In reality, the term is a bit of a

⬇ An active convective cell, just developing a hint of softness at its top, and thus becoming cumulonimbus calvus. *(Author)*

misnomer, because *calvus* is Latin for 'bald'.) This change occurs when the water droplets in the cloud begin to freeze into ice crystals.

Cumulonimbus capillatus (Cb cap) forms as more ice crystals form at the tops of the rising cells, gradually changing from the soft calvus form, to become noticeably fibrous in appearance (*capillatus* is the Latin for 'hairy'). The ice crystals may fall more-or-less vertically, giving a striated appearance to the top of the cloud, or they may fall into clear air beneath, and be seen as fallstreaks (virga).

Sometimes the crystals are carried horizontally and spread out into an overhanging anvil. On other occasions, particularly if the winds are very strong at that level, a vast cirrus plume may form, which is rapidly carried downwind.

VARIETIES OF CUMULONIMBUS CLOUD

There are no cumulonimbus varieties, but there are four accessory clouds and several supplementary features, described in the following sections.

⬇ A cumulonimbus cloud, with a cirrus plume that showed explosive growth. *(Author)*

Accessory clouds

Although none of these accessory clouds occur exclusively with cumulonimbus, many are most commonly associated with this cloud type. Cumulonimbus is, in fact, the only type in which all might occur simultaneously.

Accessory cloud types

- Flumen
- Pannus
- Pileus
- Velum

↑ Pileus: a layer of humid air, lifted to its dew point by a rising convective cell. *(Author)*

Flumen is a band of cloud that flows inwards toward the main cloud base. It is generally only seen with major storms, particularly with supercell storms.

Pannus is ragged shreds of cloud beneath the main cloud base. Such patches of cloud arise when the air below the main cloud becomes saturated with moisture, causing condensation to occur.

Pileus is a cap of cloud, consisting of a humid layer that is pushed up by a strongly rising convective cell beneath it. A pileus layer (also known as a cap cloud) eventually becomes incorporated into the main cloud mass.

Velum is a shallow, but extensive, horizontal layer of cloud that tends to lie above the tops of cumuliform clouds, but is often penetrated by the tallest towers of cumulus congestus and cumulonimbus. It frequently persists long after the convective clouds have dissipated.

↓ A layer of velum, remaining behind following the passage of a cluster of cumulonimbus and cumulus convective cells. *(Author)*

Supplementary features

Supplementary features associated with cumulonimbus cloud

There is a wide range of different forms that clouds may take, and most of these occur with cumulonimbus clouds, so, these forms are described here. A few others that are not found with cumulonimbus are described in the following sub-section (page 89).

Those associated with cumulonimbus cloud are:

- Arcus (arc)
- Cauda (cau)
- Incus (inc)
- Mamma (mam)
- Murus (mur)
- Praecipitatio (pre)
- Tuba (tub)
- Virga (vir)

Arcus (arc) is a dense roll of cloud extending across the sky. It is found on the lower, leading edge of certain active cloud systems. It often occurs in association with cumulonimbus or the larger multicell and supercell systems, but may occasionally be seen with less vigorous cumulus clouds. The edges are often more-or-less ragged and when the cloud is particularly heavy and extensive it appears as a dark arch across the sky. (It is also known as an arch cloud, from which it derives its name.) Sometimes there is circulation within the band of cloud producing an active rolling action.

→ A shelf cloud (arcus) ahead of a major cumulonimbus cluster. Air is rising along the upper, smooth surface into the advancing cloud. *(Author)*

Cauda (cau) is a horizontal band or tail of cloud that extends towards the wall cloud (murus – see below) in certain supercell cumulonimbus systems.

Incus (inc) is a flattened anvil shape The highly characteristic 'anvil' form that occurs only with cumulonimbus clouds (cumulonimbus incus). Anvils develop when the cloud reaches a major inversion, often at the tropopause. The ice crystals at the top of the cloud are carried sideways, producing the flattened cirrus shield. Generally, with strong convection, the cloud does expand slightly upwind, but most of the crystals are carried downwind, leading to the classic anvil shape. Mamma (see next feature) often develop beneath the overhanging anvil.

Mamma (mam) are pouches or bulges beneath a cloud (the name comes from the Latin word for 'udder'). Although perhaps most common beneath cumulonimbus anvils, they are also occasionally found with cirrus, cirrocumulus, altocumulus, altostratus, and stratocumulus. A localised

↑ Mamma beneath a cumulonimbus anvil. *(Author)*

↑ This tuba has now reached the sea, becoming a waterspout, and raised a cloud of spray. *(Mike Spenkman)*

downdraught carries cold air down into a warmer layer, causing it to cool to its dewpoint and produce cloud droplets. This process has been termed 'upside-down convection'.

The mamma seen beneath many types of cloud are relatively small and not particularly pronounced, but beneath cumulonimbus clouds they may assume various forms and are sometimes extremely striking, particularly if they are illuminated by low rays of light from the Sun. Beneath the main body of a cloud, they may appear as long, distorted tubes, but beneath a cumulonimbus anvil they often appear as enormous globular masses. Occasionally mamma may persist even after the main cumulonimbus cloud and the cirrus anvil have decayed and disappeared.

Murus (mur) is a wall cloud: a well-defined (and often sudden) lowering of the rain-free base of a supercell storm and is a region of very strong updraught. It often exhibits strong rotation, and may give rise to funnel clouds (tuba – see below) or tornadoes.

Praecipitatio (pre) is essentially rain, snow or hail reaching the ground. Praecipitatio (precipitation) is associated with many

different cloud genera, and it may be in the form of rain, hail or snow, but in all cases the precipitation reaches the surface, and does not evaporate into the air beneath the cloud, unlike the situation with virga (see below). The term covers everything from drizzle or a light dusting of snow to torrential rain and destructive hail. It most commonly applies to nimbostratus, cumulus congestus, and cumulonimbus, but – depending on circumstances – may also be encountered with altostratus, stratocumulus, and stratus. It is closely related to virga, another supplementary feature.

Tuba (tub) is any form of funnel cloud that descends from an active cloud. If it touches down on the surface it may become known by another term, such as waterspout, landspout or tornado.

Virga (vir) is the formal term for fallstreaks, which are trails of precipitation that descend from a cloud, but which evaporate before reaching the ground. They are associated with many different genera of clouds – in fact, with any that may produce rain, hail or snow.

Supplementary features not associated with cumulonimbus cloud

There are a few supplementary features that are not associated with cumulonimbus clouds, but with other genera, and which are described below:

- Asperitas (asp)
- Cavum (cav)
- Fluctus (flu)

⬆ A cavum in the form of a long trail, or distrail. *(Author)*

Asperitas (asp) describes the appearance of the underside of stratocumulus or altocumulus, where there are distinct wave or it seems rough. (The word *asperitas* is Latin for 'unevenness' or 'roughness'.)

Cavum (cav) is an approximately circular (or linear) hole in a layer of altocumulus, cirrocumulus or even stratocumulus cloud. Such holes, also known as 'fallstreak holes' or 'hole punch clouds', arise when an aircraft has passed through the layer, initiating the formation of ice crystals, which fall out, leaving the hole. Frequently trails of crystals in the form of fallstreaks

⬇ Passage of an aircraft through this thin layer of altocumulus has probably initiated glaciation in the cloud. The ice crystals have fallen out, creating the cavum and producing a dense patch of cirrus beneath it. *(Author)*

(virga), may be seen below the cloud. On occasions, when an aircraft has flown at the same height as the layer for an extended period, the 'hole' may be in the form of a line, sometimes known as a 'distrail'.

Fluctus (flu) is an uncommon feature when the upper surface of a cloud layer appears in the form of waves. These waves or curls may seem to be 'breaking', but in reality arise from horizontal wind shear at that level. They are also known as Kelvin-Helmholtz waves, but are extremely short-lived, generally lasting just seconds to perhaps a couple of minutes.

⬇ This train of Kelvin-Helmholtz wave clouds above San Francisco Bay was visible for just a short period of time. *(Peggy Duly)*

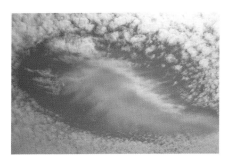

Nacreous clouds

Even higher than the three genera that are described as high-level clouds, on occasion brilliantly multi-coloured displays of cloud are seen in the west at sunset or in the east at sunrise. These are the nacreous clouds.

Generally, such displays are seen only at fairly high latitudes, greater than about 50°N or S, when the sky itself is reasonably dark and the observers are in twilight. The clouds are visible because they are illuminated by sunlight when lower clouds are in darkness. The pastel colours generally visible in the clouds are extremely striking and such displays usually generate

Key features of nacreous clouds

- Beautifully coloured, high-altitude clouds, appearing very similar to cirrocumulus lenticularis (see page 80), seen against a dark sky shortly after sunset or before sunrise.
- A colourless form is seen on rare occasions, and occurs only under specific circumstances.

considerable public interest and are widely reported in the media. Occasionally (and under specific circumstances) a white form is observed. Although displays before dawn are just as common as those occurring in the evening, they are less widely reported, simply because fewer observers are then awake.

The clouds are known as nacreous or 'mother-of-pearl' clouds because of their beautiful display of pastel shades. The more technical name is 'polar stratospheric clouds' (or PSC). As the latter name suggests, they occur in the stratosphere at altitudes of 15–30km. The stratosphere is normally extremely dry, but with the extremely low temperatures that occur in late autumn, winter, and early spring, clouds may sometimes form.

As with iridescence, the bands of colour in the clouds show the location of similarly sized particles. The clouds arise when there is rapid uplift of air by atmospheric

Nacreous clouds sky effects

The pastel colours normally seen in nacreous clouds greatly resemble those found with iridescence (see page 102) and arise from the same mechanism: diffraction of sunlight by tiny particles in the clouds. In the case of nacreous clouds, the particles may have a complex composition and contain nitric acid trihydrate, sulphuric acid, nitric acid or water (the exact composition enables specialists to divide these clouds into various categories). Some of these chemical compounds are the result of material ejected into the atmosphere by volcanoes. The sulphuric acid droplets, for example, result from the reaction of volcanic sulphur dioxide gas with water molecules.

↑ Brilliantly coloured nacreous clouds, February 2016. *(Ken Kennedy)*

waves, normally caused by mountains on the surface. The abrupt cooling of the air produces large quantities of similarly sized droplets or water-ice crystals. The much rarer, white form of cloud is more commonly observed in the southern hemisphere over Antarctica. There, the clouds are similar wave clouds, and arise when the air flowing in persistent winds is subject to a very slow drop in temperature. This often occurs at the beginning of the winter season. The particles consist of water ice with a core of nitric acid hydrate, but because they form slowly are much larger in size. As a result they diffract a whole range of wavelengths, rather than a specific narrow range. Rather than the particles showing a particular colour, they thus appear white, although there is sometimes a hint of colour around the edges of the clouds.

Nacreous clouds and the ozone layer

Nacreous clouds are involved in the formation of ozone holes, where the ozone layer in the upper stratosphere is depleted in ozone and ceases to function as a screen to block damaging solar ultraviolet radiation from reaching the ground. The clouds cause this effect because the surfaces of the particles provide a location for the various photochemical reactions that destroy ozone. The reactions are particularly strong over the Antarctic with the return of sunlight in the spring and are the cause of the major, persistent ozone hole over Antarctica. Conditions over the Arctic are less consistent, and although depletion of ozone does occur, any resulting ozone holes are relatively short-lived and do not occur every year.

Noctilucent clouds

As mentioned earlier, the very highest clouds in the atmosphere, even higher than the nacreous clouds described previously, are those known as noctilucent (Latin: 'night-shining') clouds, commonly abbreviated 'NLC'.

They occur high in the mesosphere, at about the level of the mesopause (see page 29). These clouds are seen during the summer, for about five or six weeks before and after the summer solstice. They are generally visible from latitudes between 50 and 70° north and south of the equator, when they are visible only in the direction of the pole. Although at such high latitudes twilight conditions persist throughout the night, noctilucent clouds are highly distinctive and readily recognised. They are visible because they are at such great altitudes that they remain illuminated by sunlight, even though the Sun itself is below the polar horizon, and the observer is in darkness. The clouds occur at altitudes of between 75 and 85km, which is somewhat below the actual mesopause altitude, which, in summer is about 100km near the poles. There are suggestions that ice crystals form near the mesopause and fall down to the lower level at which the clouds are visible.

The clouds exist as a thin layer – there are suggestions that sometimes there are two layers – and the structures primarily arise because of undulations in the layer. These undulations are, perhaps

⬇ Noctilucent clouds, photographed from Tarbatness, Ross-shire. *(Denis Buczynski)*

Noctilucent clouds

"...weird small cloud forms, at times very regular, like ripple marks in sand, or the bones of some great fish or saurian embedded on a slab of stone."

Robert Leslie (*Nature* 1884)

surprisingly, caused by what are known as gravity (or buoyancy) waves: waves created far below by the flow of air over mountains on the surface. The waves propagate up through the atmosphere, but are only apparent when NLC are present. The visible structure and apparent changes in density arise because of variations in the number of particles along the line of sight. In general, the layer of cloud is so thin that it

Key features of noctilucent clouds

- Generally visible from latitudes between 50 and 70° north and south of the equator, when they are visible only in the direction of the pole, during darkness/twilight conditions.
- Seen during the summer, for about five or six weeks before and after the summer solstice.
- In general, the clouds have a distinctive, electric-blue colour, although this may be tinged with yellow both early in the night and towards dawn.

The formation of noctilucent clouds

Very little is known about the way in which noctilucent clouds form. They are known to consist of ice crystals, and satellite observations indicate that they form at very low temperatures from water vapour and 'dust' particles, but there is great disagreement about the origins of the water vapour and the 'dust'.

There is the question of how the water vapour reaches such great altitudes. There is no definitely known mechanism by which water vapour could be transported from the surface upwards to such great altitudes, although it has been suggested that water vapour could filter through 'gaps' in the tropopause, which otherwise acts as a water-vapour 'trap'. One idea has been that the water was of cosmic origin, brought by cometary ice particles. Recently it has been suggested that the water vapour might be produced in the stratosphere in reactions between methane and hydroxyl radicals and then diffuse upwards into the mesosphere.

As for the 'dust', it appears highly unlikely that any material – such as that ejected by volcanoes – could be transported to such great altitudes. But an ice crystal requires a seed particle, a solid nucleus, on which to form (see page 20). One suggestion is that the nuclei consist of meteoric particles from space. Another is that the nuclei are clusters of ions that have been created by incoming cosmic rays.

↑ NLC of Type I (Veil). *(Ken Kennedy)*

is invisible when directly above any observer, yet it may be clearly visible to other observers at a distance.

A noctilucent cloud display often shows a drift towards the west-south-west (in the northern hemisphere), carried along by the generally easterly upper-atmosphere winds. However, the characteristic structures often appear to move in the opposite direction. In reality, the standing waves, generated far below at the surface, that have propagated up through the atmosphere, generally remain stationary, when conditions at the surface are unchanging.

Noctilucent clouds and aurorae

Because aurorae (see page 96) cause heating of the upper atmosphere, it was believed for many years that noctilucent clouds could not form when there was a major auroral display. In the late 20th century however, a Canadian amateur managed to photograph both occurring simultaneously, and other such images have been obtained subsequently. Any auroral heating is obviously occurring at a different altitude and thus not destroying the ice crystals in the clouds.

TYPES OF NOCTILUCENT CLOUD

Although noctilucent clouds often appear disorganised, certain distinctive forms are frequently observed, and there are four main structural versions, which are known as 'Types'.

Unfortunately, a single type is rarely seen on its own, and normally more than one occurs during a display. Frequently, only observation during an event will reveal how a particular type has developed. Various subdivisions and more complex forms are recognised by specialist observers. Bright knots may occur, for example, where two sets of bands cross one another.

The four types are:

- **Type I: Veils** are tenuous films, resembling cirrus or cirrostratus, sometimes with a slight fibrous structure. These often precede, or occur as a background to other forms.
- **Type II: Bands** are long streaks, often in groups that are approximately parallel, but sometimes crossing at a shallow angle. They may change in brightness over periods of 20–60 minutes.
- **Type III: Billows** are closely spaced,

↑ NLC of Type II (bands), with some Type III (waves). *(Ken Kennedy)*

approximately parallel, short streaks. These sometimes appear on their own, or may cross the longer bands. Billows often change form and pattern and alter in brightness within minutes.

- **Type IV: Whirls** are partial or complete loops or rings of cloud with dark centres. Closed rings are rare.

↓ NLC, Type III (waves). *(Ken Kennedy)*

↓ NLC, Type IV (whirls), with some Type III waves. *(Ken Kennedy)*

The Aurora

Although not directly related to clouds or the weather, observers may occasionally see auroral displays in the upper atmosphere. They are even higher than the noctilucent clouds described previously.

Aurorae are most frequently visible at high latitudes, such as northern Europe (particularly Scandinavia) and Canada, or on the other side of the world, from South Island in New Zealand. On very rare occasions, when the Sun has been particularly active, displays may be seen almost anywhere on Earth. On a very few occasions displays have been seen from the Caribbean and even Singapore.

The ionosphere

The ionosphere consists of part of the thermosphere above 60–70km and extending out to about 1,000km, well into the exosphere. Here, ultraviolet and X-ray radiation from the Sun ionises atoms in the rarefied atmosphere (they are stripped of one or more electrons). The ionisation creates high electrical conductivity and this has two main results. Certain radio wavelengths from space are prevented from reaching the surface, so research in these wavelength-regions must be carried out by satellites, orbiting at greater heights. The other effect is that certain radio wavelengths from the ground are reflected and thus enable long-distance communications. Both effects are sometimes disrupted by the ejection of masses of charged material from the Sun, which impact on the upper atmosphere and alter the properties of the ionosphere, sometimes giving rise to aurorae.

What is an aurora?

Auroral displays occur when energetic particles are emitted by violent events on the Sun. When these particles reach the Earth and cascade into the upper atmosphere, into what is known as the ionosphere, they raise the energy level of the atoms or molecules of gas that are present. These excited atoms or molecules then radiate away the excess

⬇ One of Fridjof Nansen's auroral paintings.

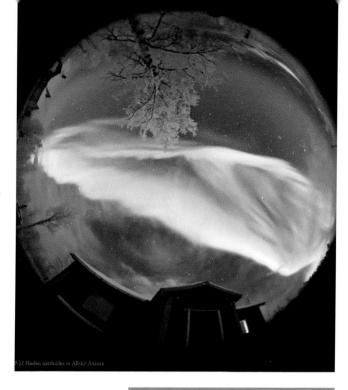

→ All-sky image of the aurora. *(P-M. Heden)*

energy in the form of light, giving rise to an auroral display. The transitions give rise to very specific colours.

Auroral events occur at any time of the day or night, but are, of course, only readily visible during night-time. At dawn and dusk, the tops of energetic displays may be illuminated by direct sunlight, giving rise to the violet tints, which are less common around local midnight. It should be noted that photographs, because they gather light over an interval of time – however short – often show far more detail than is visible to the eye. So do not be disappointed if an auroral display does not live up to expectations. The photographs included here have been chosen to show typical displays, not the extremely dramatic images that have sometimes been captured during major auroral displays.

Observers who are favourably placed to observe the aurora frequently – ie, those who live in suitable northern latitudes – sometimes make use of special all-sky cameras to record events. These can sometime produce dramatic images of the sky during a display.

Aurorae take place in the ionosphere, far above the regions where normal clouds

Aurora borealis and aurora australis

During magnetic storms, the Earth's magnetic field tends to funnel energetic particles from the Sun into regions around the magnetic poles, one of which lies in the high Canadian Arctic, and the other in the Antarctic. Auroral displays occur in the auroral zones, which are approximately 15–30° from the magnetic poles. The area in which a particular auroral display is taking place at any one time is known as the auroral oval. Displays in the north (the Northern Lights) are known as the aurora borealis and those in the south (the Southern Lights) as the aurora australis. Major displays often occur simultaneously in both northern and southern regions.

Aurora colours

The colours that people see depend greatly on their individual eyesight, with some people unable to see the reddish tints, for example. The most commonly reported colour is green, emitted by oxygen atoms, followed by red from nitrogen molecules. A violet colour is sometimes seen when extremely long auroral rays extend high in the atmosphere and are illuminated by direct sunlight. Very weak aurorae may appear almost colourless, because the eye is unable to detect colour at low light levels. In past centuries, bright red aurorae have often been taken for the signs of distant conflagrations, to the extent that troops have been sent to fight non-existent fires.

⬇ Aurora with violet rays, Tarbatness, Ross-shire. *(Denis Buczynski)*

⬇ An aurora with a bright red section, Tarbatness, Ross-shire. *(Denis Buczynski)*

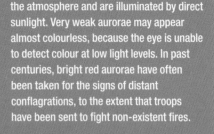

occur, most commonly at altitudes of between 70 and 300km, but may occasionally extend up to 1,000km or more. There are various distinctive auroral forms, although certain forms – especially those seen late in a display – may sometimes be mistaken for clouds illuminated by distant lights.

The occurrence of aurorae closely follows the so-called sunspot cycle, which is actually a cycle of solar activity, which waxes and wanes over a period of approximately 11 years. Most aurorae occur when the Sun is highly active and this may occur at any time of year. At high latitudes (Northern Europe, Siberia, Canada, and Antarctica), aurorae are naturally invisible during the long summer twilight – but this is exactly the time when observers should be alert for the presence of noctilucent clouds (see page 92). For many years it was considered impossible for aurorae and noctilucent clouds to occur at the same time, because aurorae create heating of the upper atmosphere, and would thus prevent the ice crystals of noctilucent clouds from forming. However, it is now known that this view was incorrect and both phenomena have been observed simultaneously on numerous occasions, mainly because they occur at very different heights.

Forms of aurorae

There are several major auroral forms, and some (or all) of these may be seen during the course of a major display.

Form	Abbr.	Description
Arc	A	Arch-like structure, highest in direction of the pole; distinct lower edge
Band	B	Deep ribbon-like structure, folded like curtains
Corona	C	Broad rays that appear to radiate from a point overhead
Ray	R	An approximately vertical streak of light
Glow	G	A weak glow on the horizon
Patch	P	A luminous area, resembling a cloud
Veil	V	A faint, even glow across a large area of sky

Additionally, there are two sub-divisions of arcs and bands to differentiate different forms. These are:

- **Homogeneous (H)** – without any notable structure, but usually evenly graduated from a bright, distinct lower edge to a faint, diffuse upper border
- **Rayed (R)** – distinct, vertical striations, with individual rays often extending beyond the main area of luminosity

A homogeneous arc is thus reported as HA, and a rayed band as RB. Experienced observers also add codes to indicate colours, rapidity of motion, and include measurements of the altitude of parts of the display above the horizon. An approximate estimate of the altitude of the

⬇ A typical homogenous arc aurora, Tarbatness, Ross-shire. *(Denis Buczynski)*

↑ A strongly rayed arc. *(Denis Buczynski)*

base of an arc or band may be made by eye, using the methods described elsewhere (see page 119).

The evolution of an auroral display

Although auroral displays often begin as a glow or veil – and thus frequently go un-noticed, the most commonly seen form is a homogenous arc. This will often develop rays, and in a particularly active display will go on to show bands – like waving curtains of light – or else the rays will extend high into the sky, sweep overhead and become a corona. (This term must not be confused the optical corona often observed in clouds – see page 102 – which arises from a completely different cause.)

← A very typical auroral patch, Tarbatness, Ross-shire. *(Denis Buczynski)*

↙ Auroral curtains, Tarbatness, Ross-shire. *(Denis Buczynski)*

↓ An auroral corona, Tarbatness, Ross-shire. *(Denis Buczynski)*

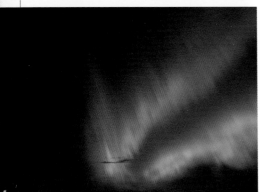

Colours in the clouds

Clouds obviously sometimes show dramatic colours at sunrise and sunset, but there are other optical effects that occur within clouds, and which are often missed.

The colours seen in clouds (with which we also include fog and mist) fall into two broad categories, depending on whether they are created by water droplets or ice crystals.

➜ The rear of a receding front at sunrise. *(Author)*

⬇ Contrail remnants at sunset. *(Author)*

Cloud optical effects caused by water (cloud) droplets

There are three main effects caused by water (cloud) droplets:

- Iridescence
- Coronae
- Glories

IRIDESCENCE

Iridescence is seen when looking in the general directions of the Sun or Moon and is probably best seen in altocumulus clouds or the edges of altostratus. Here bands of colour run along the edges of the cloud, and the presence of a particular colour indicates the presence of particles that are all of the same size. In altocumulus, and particularly in altostratus, because they are mixed clouds, the particles may consist of either water droplets or tiny ice crystals. The pastel colours arise by a process known as diffraction, where light – usually from the Sun – is behind the cloud and is diffracted by different amounts depending on its wavelength, giving rise to the various colours. The most striking displays usually occur about 30° from the Sun.

CORONAE

Coronae is the plural term for 'corona', used here to describe a specific optical effect seen in clouds, which should not be confused with the same term as applied to aurorae (see page 96X), nor the term used to describe the outer atmosphere of the Sun.

As with iridescence, a corona is seen when looking in the general direction of the Sun or Moon. A corona appears within a cloud, surrounding the disk of the Sun or Moon. Coronae around the Moon are often easier to see than those around the Sun, which may be too bright for the colours to be seen. It may, in any

case, be necessary to hide the Sun or Moon behind some convenient object, such as a telephone pole, for a corona to be visible.

There is an inner region to a corona, and this is known as the aureole. It is a circular disk, with a reddish-brownish border. It tends to appear when the cloud droplets are fairly large. Smaller droplets

⬆ The outer rings of a corona are often strongly coloured and their shape may be slightly distorted by the structure of the cloud in which they appear. *(Author)*

tend to produce a large set of rings, which may show various strong colours. Quite frequently, only part of a set of rings is visible, depending on the shape and

⬇ The inner aureole of a corona in thin, water-droplet altocumulus clouds. *(Author)*

The Brocken Spectre

There is a famous effect associated with glories, known as the Brocken Spectre, where there appears to be a giant shadow cast onto the cloud. In fact, this is an optical illusion, caused by the fact that, because of the mistiness, the eyes cannot focus accurately on any part of the shadow, and the brain imagines that it is larger than its true size.

↑ A brilliant glory on mountain mist around the shadow of the observer's head. *(Claudia Hinz)*

density of the clouds. As with iridescence, the colours are caused by diffraction, but in this case the disk and rings are centred on the Sun or Moon, rather than some distance away from it.

GLORIES

In contrast to iridescence and coronae, glories are seen when looking directly away from the Sun. Under ideal conditions, glories have been created by moonlight, but they are very rare. A glory consists of a set of coloured rings around the shadow of the observer's head. It is usually seen when the observer is looking down onto a bank of cloud or mist. Under very favourable conditions, several sets of coloured rings may be visible.

Glories are almost certainly the origin of the haloes that some have believed to surround the heads of holy persons. If there are several observers, a single observer sees only the glory surrounding their own head.

The 22° halo

There is one common halo, which appears as a ring around the Sun, with a radius of 22°. This is equal to the spread fingers of one hand, held at arms length, as shown on page 119. It is naturally known as the 22° halo. Although the ring usually appears white, sometimes it may show tinges of colour, with red on the inside and a violet shade on the outside. Haloes may also occur around the Moon, but naturally, these tend to be fainter and more difficult to see.

Sometimes a second halo is visible, lying outside the main 22° halo. This has a radius of 46° and is usually much fainter. If any colours are visible, again they will be similar to those in the 22° halo, with a reddish tinge on the inside.

Cloud optical effects caused by ice particles

There are numerous effects that may be caused by ice particles in the atmosphere – far too many to be described in detail here. The forms that are most common include:

- ■ Halo
- ■ Parhelion (mock Sun)
- ■ Circumzenithal arc
- ■ Sun pillar

HALOES

Haloes are actually very common, but rarely noticed by casual observers. They frequently occur whenever a depression is approaching, preceded by its sheet of

high-altitude cirrostratus cloud. In Britain, this occurs, on average, once every three days, so haloes are often visible, if people only keep an eye on the sky, although haloes tend to appear when the sheet of cirrostratus is fairly thin and before it thickens or becomes fibrous in appearance.

PARHELION (MOCK SUN)

Almost as frequent as haloes are parhelia (the singular is 'parhelion') or 'mock Suns'. These frequently occur at the same time as the 22° halo, and appear as bright spots of light that lie, at the same altitude as the Sun, and seem to be at the same distance from the Sun as the halo. In reality, they lie a very small distance outside the 22° halo – too close for it to be apparent to the eye. Sometimes they show a distinct white 'tail' pointing away from the Sun. Strongly coloured parhelia also often occur in isolated patches of cirrus cloud and here, the colours are often particularly brilliant.

↑ A fine halo display in cirrostratus cloud, showing the 22° halo, a portion of the 46° halo, parhelia on both sides of the Sun, an upper arc of contact with the 22° halo, and a circumzenithal arc. *(Dave Gavine)*

↓ A bright, coloured parhelion in a patch of cirrus, with an indication of the bright 'tail' that is sometimes seen, pointing away from the Sun. *(Author)*

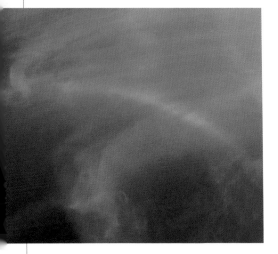

CIRCUMZENITHAL ARC

Although there are many halo arcs, the circumzenithal arc is the most common, and is the arc often described in the media as an 'upside-down rainbow'. In reality, of course, it has no connection with rainbows whatsoever, because it is created by light passing through ice crystals, not raindrops. It is usually brightly coloured. It forms a partial arc (part of a circle that is centred on the zenith). If the 46° halo is visible (see box 'The 22° halo'), the circumzenithal arc touches the very top.

SUN PILLAR

Sun pillars are fairly common, but rarely noticed. They are vertical columns of light, above and below the Sun, usually in a cirriform cloud. They are created when light from the Sun is reflected from the horizontal faces of ice crystals floating in the air.

⬆ A circumzenithal arc, seen in cirrus uncinus and a thin veil of cirrostratus. *(Author)*

⬇ A sun pillar in an extensive sheet of striated cirrus above the setting Sun. *(Author)*

Rainbows

Although rainbows do not appear in clouds, clouds (rain-clouds) are obviously essential for them to appear. Similarly, the Sun must be shining on the falling rain.

Light from the Sun is reflected back towards the observer by the rear surfaces of the falling raindrops, and the light is refracted within the raindrops, causing it to spread out into the spectral colours.

The most common rainbow is known as the primary bow, with red on the outside and violet on the inner edge. The red arc has a radius of 42°, and the violet edge a radius of 40°. The elevation of the top of a rainbow depends solely on the elevation of the Sun, because a rainbow is centred on what is known as the antisolar point – the point in the sky, directly opposite the Sun. The higher the Sun, the lower the top of the rainbow. When the Sun is on the horizon, a rainbow may appear as a full semi-circle and, indeed, when seen from an aircraft or (sometimes) from a mountain-top, a rainbow may appear as a complete circle.

The secondary bow

Quite frequently, a second bow, the secondary bow, is seen outside the primary bow, but with a reversed sequence of colours. This time the radius of the inner, red edge is 52°, and that of the outer, violet edge is 54°. This bow arises from a double reflection within each raindrop.

The region between the primary and secondary bows normally appears much darker than the surrounding sky. This known as Alexander's dark band, and arises because the light in this region is directed away from the observer's eyes.

Pastel-coloured arcs

Occasionally, pastel-coloured arcs appear inside the primary bow. These usually appear as narrow bands with some colour, often violet and pale green in tint. These are known as supernumery bows (or interference bows) and occur because light has taken slightly different paths through the raindrops.

Rainbow brightness

The strength of colours in rainbows may vary considerably. Generally, the larger the raindops, the brigher the bows. However, a lot depends on the colour of the light from the Sun. At sunset or sunrise, that light may be predominantly red, and then only red rainbows are observed.

⬇ A double rainbow, photographed in New South Wales. This display is a little unusual in that the area between the primary and secondary bows (Alexander's Dark Band) is no darker than the sky outside the secondary bow. *(Duncan Waldron)*

Fogbows

When the droplets are very small, as in mist or fog, then no colours are visible, merely a white arc. Such white bows are known as fogbows.

"There's joy in the mountains;
There's life in the fountains;
Small clouds are sailing,
Blue sky prevailing;
The rain is over and gone!"

William Wordsworth, *Written in March*, 1801

Chapter 5
Clouds and weather

Although particular types of cloud are not necessarily infallible signs of changes in the weather, some are definitely associated with changes that may occur, or may be indicators of immediately imminent weather conditions. The most typical example is how the gradual change of cloud type ahead of an approaching depression is a sure sign that major changes in the weather are likely to occur.

← Heavy rain from a cumulonimbus cloud. *(Shutterstock)*

The depression sequence

The first signs of an approaching depression come with the early high clouds at the tip of a warm front (see the diagram on page 26). Although there are some variations, depending on the strength of the approaching depression, the general sequence of clouds is:

1 Cirrus wisps
2 Cirrostratus
3 Altostratus
4 Nimbostratus

Normally, the first to arrive are wisps of high cirrus, which gradually invade the sky. An even earlier sign that is sometimes seen is the presence of jet-stream cirrus, racing east on westerly winds. This jet stream is approximately parallel to the approaching warm front. Although such jet-stream clouds may sometimes occur behind a depression (behind the cold front), they are then normally moving north or north-east, driven by southerly winds.

As the cirrus wisps gradually thicken into a sheet of cirrocumulus, at the surface convection slowly decreases, and the increasing warm air at altitude produces an inversion. Convection is suppressed and any cumulus clouds tend to become flattened: cumulus humilis.

Initially, the sheet of cirrostratus may the thin enough to show haloes (see page 104) but as it thickens (usually becoming streaked, or 'striated') it lowers and turns into altostratus, the Sun becomes hidden and as if seen through ground glass. Objects on the ground no longer cast shadows. Sometimes, for a short period, scattered altocumulus (see Chapter 4) may

⬇ Jet-stream cirrus forms highly distinctive bands of cloud across the sky. *(Author)*

Cloud sequence for a cold front

The sequence of clouds is less clear-cut at a cold front (see the diagram on page 26), largely because the immediate approach of the front is masked by any existing cloud. However, because the front is steeper than a warm front, there is a similar, reversed, sequence of clouds, which occurs more rapidly. With an active depression, cumulonimbus clouds may occur along the line of the front, giving heavy bursts of rain. Behind a cold front there is usually a transition to clear, cold air with scattered heavy showers.

appear before the cloud sheet turns into unbroken altostratus.

Finally, the altostratus lowers and thickens still further, and the cloud becomes nimbostratus, bringing more-or-less continuous rain.

With weak depressions (which are quite common over Britain), the cloud may never develop into heavy nimbostratus. Instead, the cloud may become heavy stratocumulus, with only drizzle or very light rain (if any).

The distribution of the different types of cloud in a typical active depression is highly characteristic. The exact sequence of clouds seen will, however, depend on where the observer is located relative to the centre of the depression. Between the warm front and the advancing cold front (see diagram on page 26) there is an area known as the warm sector, where the cloud cover may be quite broken. Quite often, however, the clouds here may be extensive stratocumulus.

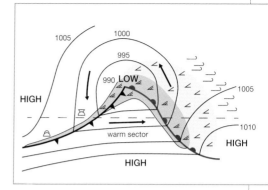

⬆The overall pattern of rain in a depression, before any occluded front has formed. *(Ian Moores)*

⬇A satellite image (obtained with amateur equipment) of two depressions. The larger has a poorly defined warm front and warm sector, but shows a distinct 'clear slot' behind the cold front, which is missing from the smaller and weaker, earlier depression at top right. Both show extensive convective cloud in the cold polar maritime air. *(Author)*

Let it snow!

Although the characteristic feature of most depressions is that they bring long periods of rain, when conditions are suitable they may, of course, give rise to large quantities of snow. This is particularly the case when air temperatures at the surface are low, perhaps because cold air has previously invaded the area. Sometimes, when the air at the surface is particularly cold, rain falling from the nimbostratus clouds may freeze on impact with the ground, giving rise to an ice storm (see page 22).

Showers

Although amateur observers may regard any short burst of rain as a 'shower', to meteorologists the term is used to refer to the distinctive periods of rain from strong convective (usually cumulonimbus, or occasionally cumulus congestus) clouds.

Giant cumulonimbus clouds reach so far into the high atmosphere that their tops reach temperatures well below freezing and any water droplets turn to ice – the technical term is that the tops become

glaciated. The resulting rain is known as 'cold rain' (see box, 'Cold rain and warm rain'), in distinction from the 'warm rain' that falls from tropical clouds and, sometimes in summer, in temperate regions, from cumulus congestus or cumulonimbus clouds.

The vigorous convection that occurs within cumulonimbus clouds carries large quantities of humid air high into the atmosphere, where it freezes, and produces large amounts of rain. The powerful updraughts reach high into the cloud, and the falling rain creates corresponding downdraughts. The lifetime of shower clouds is limited because eventually the downdraughts quench the rising updraughts, thus cutting off the supply of humid air and causing the rain to die away.

The powerful downdraughts within cumulonimbus clouds reach the ground and fan out ahead of the approaching cloud. These apparent winds flowing out of the cloud are often the reason why people say that a shower 'approached against the wind'. So there are strong currents of air flowing into, and also out from, an active cumulonimbus cloud. Usually the inflowing air rises above the cold outflow, and may produce some of the supplementary

← Roll and shelf clouds, created by strong up- and downdraughts ahead of an advancing, very active cumulonimbus cloud. *(Author)*

↑ A column of heavy rain from the mature stage of a single cumulonimbus cell. Eventually the downdraught will quench the updraught of warm, humid air feeding the cloud, and the rain will cease. *(Duncan Waldron)*

features (such as arcus – see page 87) that are sometimes seen.

The evolution of a shower cloud

The lifetime of a shower cloud occurs in three stages:

- **Early**: cumulus congestus
- **Middle**: cumulonimbus calvus and cumulonimbus capillatus, possibly with development of an anvil (incus)
- **Late**: gradual decay of the cloud and declining precipitation

The first two stages each last about 20 minutes. During the latter part of the second (middle) stage, rainfall is heaviest. The final (late) stage may last anywhere between about 30 minutes and two hours.

Cold rain and warm rain

Rain may be produced by two different processes in the atmosphere: processes known (somewhat faceciously) as cold rain and warm rain.

At temperate latitudes, the most common way rain forms is through what is known as 'cold rain'. In this process, ice crystals form in high in clouds – particularly cumulonimbus – and as these ice crystals fall into warmer layers, they melt into raindrops.

The other process can only occur when clouds are very deep and turbulent. In such clouds, the tiny cloud droplets collide and gradually grow large enough to start to fall as raindrops. This is 'warm rain' – because no ice crystals form – and often occurs in clouds in the tropics. It may also take place in very deep cumulus congestus clouds in summer in more temperate regions.

Thunderstorms

Cumulonimbus clouds are, of course, the source of lightning and its associated thunder. The exact causes of the separation of charges that leads to lightning is still uncertain, but it is known to involve the freezing process, when the lightest, positively charged particles are carried to the top of the cloud, while the heavier, negatively charged particles migrate towards the base of the cloud. There, they induce a positive charge on the ground below, and that charge moves across the landscape, following the movement of the cloud. When the distance between the cloud and any object on the ground is sufficiently small, an electrical discharge (the lightning) takes place between the two, creating the rapid expansion and contraction of the air that produces the thunder.

⬇ A lightning strike to the sea at dusk, clearly showing the branched structure, typical of 'fork' lightning, together with the main channel through which the main discharge occurred. A strike from an unrelated active cell is visible on the left. *(Duncan Waldron)*

Hail

Sometimes the updraught within cumulonimbus cloud is so strong that it creates a 'vault' within the cloud. This is the location where hail tends to form. Falling raindrops are captured by the strongly rising air, are carried upwards and freeze. They then start to fall again, and may even start to melt. But they can be caught once again and tossed high into the cloud. This may happen several times. At the highest, freezing levels, air is usually trapped within the ice, but when the ice has melted to water, it gives a clear layer when it refreezes. So hailstones that have made several trips up and down within a cloud consist of layers of clear and opaque ice.

Funnel clouds

The strong up- and downdraughts within cumulonimbus clouds sometimes produce funnel clouds (tuba, see page 88), which hang down from the base of the clouds. If such funnels touch down to the surface, they become (depending on the actual surface) waterspouts or landspouts, or even more destructive tornadoes.

Multicell and supercell storms

Active cumulonimbus clouds may cluster together to produce what are known as multicell storms, which may persist for many hours as they travel across the countryside, even though the individual cells within them have a limited lifetime. Large systems, known as supercells, may also arise, and these usually take the form of a giant rotating system of clouds. It is these supercell systems that produce the most damaging swathes of hail, and may also be the source of highly destructive tornadoes.

Chapter 6

Observing and photographing clouds

The preceding chapters have explained how clouds are formed, classified and identified, and the influence they have on the weather. This chapter provides advice on how best to observe clouds, and how to record what you see using a camera, which is not always as straightforward as it may seem.

→ Modern digital cameras are ideal for photographing clouds, though it pays to be careful with settings. *(Shutterstock)*

"I never saw a man who looked
So wistfully at the day.
I never saw a man who looked
With such a wistful eye
Upon that little tent of blue
Which prisoners call the sky,
And at every drifting cloud that went
With sails of silver by."

Oscar Wilde, *The Ballad of
Reading Gaol*, 1897

Observing clouds

Because clouds may change so quickly and more-or-less continuously, frequent observation of the sky helps with identification of any type of cloud, and especially those that develop from other forms. So the first rule of observing clouds is: look at the sky as often as possible.

The way in which certain types change into others – sometimes going through a particular sequence of types – is often a sure sign of how the weather will develop. The best example of this is the way in which an advancing depression is foretold by wisps of high cirrus that thicken into a sheet of cirrostratus, which then thickens and lowers into altostratus, which itself then turns into nimbostratus and its accompanying rain. Noting the signs of instability at a certain height is also an indication that thunderstorms and other severe weather may develop, either later in the day or even on the next day.

Equipment for observations

Little is needed to make observations of clouds beyond a pair of binoculars and possibly a polariser. It is also useful to be able to estimate angles in the sky – see box opposite.

Angles in the sky

It is useful to be able to make approximate estimates of angles in the sky. It is easy enough to make useful estimates by holding one's hand at arm's length as shown in the diagram. This is a useful way of determining whether, for example, a cloud should be considered high stratocumulus or low altocumulus or, similarly, whether it is high altocumulus or low cirrocumulus. The differences are described in Chapter 4, on pages 67 and 79. It is also useful in determining which of the many optical phenomena may be present.

↓ Estimating angles in the sky. *(Ian Moores)*

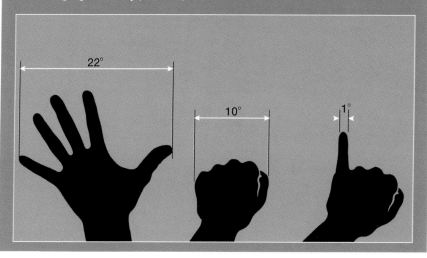

BINOCULARS

Occasionally, it may be useful to examine clouds more closely by using binoculars. These can help to reveal, for example, how a the top of a cumulonimbus cloud is changing into a calvus or capillatus species (see pages 84–85). Although not necessary for the identification of a lenticular cloud, close examination may show the slight changes as the cloud forms on the windward side and disperses to leeward.

← A sheet of altocumulus stratiformis behind a receding depression, illumated by the setting Sun. *(Author)*

POLARISER

The actual structure of clouds may become clearer if they are viewed through a polariser. This is an essential accessory for photographing clouds, but is also useful when held in front of the eye. A polariser used for observations doesn't have to be optically perfect, like a photographic filter. Thin sheets of plastic polarising material are readily available. Held in front of the eye and rotated to different angles, they will help to make the depth and structure of the cloud more readily visible. They may even reveal that what looks like one cloud is actually two forms at different distances.

Photographing clouds

It pays to always carry a camera if you are interested in clouds. Some features and optical effects – such as certain halo arcs, and Kelvin-Helmholtz waves (the form known as fluctus – see page 89) are so rare or short-lived, that a photograph with even the simplest camera may be of considerable interest. Modern digital cameras are ideal (including those in smartphones), but even the old-fashioned film cameras still have a part to play – and film is preferred by some professional photographers.

Cameras

Although some smartphone cameras are able to provide images of excellent quality, and have a surprising range of controls, they are generally limited in the type of features that they offer. In most cases, however, even the simplest compact digital camera offers more features that may help to secure a really good image. In general, a digital single-lens reflex (DSLR) camera has similar settings, but normally covers a much greater range and has greater flexibility.

With any camera it is important to study the manual to ensure that you are familiar with all the different settings that may be required to obtain the best pictures. The actual paper manuals supplied with most cameras nowadays are inadequate, and it pays to download a full manual from the manufacturer's website. Although camera manufacturers often claim that all you need do is 'point and shoot', and this may indeed help you capture a fleeting effect, generally the best images will require some adjustment to the settings before the photograph is taken. Not everything can be corrected by later work on the image, using a computer.

It usually pays to experiment with different settings. With digital images it is easy to try different approaches and then discard any images that are incorrect or do not show the effect desired. It is, however, important to be aware of the limitations of any image-processing software that may have come with the camera. It is sometimes necessary to adjust the contrast or brightness of an image, so that details are more easily seen, but the colour balance should remain unchanged. It may otherwise be difficult to appreciate the true beauty of the clouds. Too frequently, processed images are produced with brown skies or other lurid tints that are never seen in nature. Striking colours do sometimes occur on clouds and in the sky, and these should be rendered as naturally as possible.

Settings

Generally, compact and the more sophisticated DSLR cameras offer a range of settings – usually described as 'scenes', or sometimes 'modes' – for particular types of subject. The most useful for cloud photography are the landscape, snow/ beach and sunrise/sunset settings. Under most circumstances, these settings will produce acceptable, aesthetically pleasing images. The landscape setting is usually fairly satisfactory for cloud photographs, but if clouds are in full sunlight and are brilliantly white, the snow/beach setting may give better results. This is because of

→ Clouds sometimes show extreme contrasts in brightness. *(Author)*

the way in which the exposure is adjusted. Even better is the use of the High Dynamic Range (HDR) setting available with some DSLR cameras. This will satisfactorily capture the wide range of brightness that may be present with brilliantly lit clouds in one part of the image and very dark areas (such as the landscape beneath heavy clouds) in another portion.

The red and orange colours of sunrise and sunset are normally better rendered with the special sunrise/sunset scene setting. Without such a setting any automatic white-balance feature in the camera may sense that the colour temperature is now lower, and make adjustments towards a 'midday' scene, giving colours that do not match those seen by the eye. It may be possible to set some cameras to make multiple exposures at different white-balance settings and you can then choose the most satisfactory image. If, however, you intend to carry out extensive image processing using a computer, it is best to use the RAW setting that is available on most DSLR cameras, where the image is captured 'as is', without any processing within the camera itself.

It is important to ensure that any flash is turned off. On some cameras it is turned on automatically whenever a scene setting is changed. Although, naturally, a flash cannot illuminate clouds or the sky, if the flash is set to operate it may affect the exposure that the camera assumes to be correct, resulting in a less-than-optimum image. Occasionally, a 'sport' setting may be useful, if, for example, you are trying to photograph clouds over a stormy sea with fast-moving waves.

Field of view
DSLR cameras with a range of interchangeable lenses offer the most flexibility. Many compact cameras offer optical zooms with 'wide-angle' and 'telephoto' options. Some cameras may have an optical zoom and an additional 'super' or 'digital' zoom range. A digital

⬇ Sunset over the sea. *(Author)*

Photographing noctilucent clouds and aurorae

Noctilucent clouds (NLC – described on page 92) are often faint, so it pays to set a higher equivalent ISO speed – perhaps 1000 – on digital cameras, if this is possible, and to use longer exposures. Photographing the aurora (see page 96) requires fairly short exposures, because of the fairly rapid changes that occur in the display. For such images, an ISO 'speed' setting of 400 is usually satisfactory. For aurorae try a range of exposure-times: 15–30 seconds at the largest possible aperture (such as f/1.8 if you have a suitable lens). If you want to submit a full, scientific contribution for either of these subjects, try to take exposures at specific times: 0, 15, 30 or 45 minutes past the hour. Your images may then be compared with those taken by other observers. Suitable pairs of images may be used for triangulation by which the height of NLC or aurorae may be determined accurately.

zoom, unlike an optical zoom, merely enlarges a small area of the image, losing resolution and definition as it does so. Although telephoto and wide-angle attachments may be purchased for smartphones, they are not generally very satisfactory. Often a telephoto image of part of a cloud will make a more effective image than a wider view and will help to reveal the structure of a cloud, or how it is changing. Most clouds can be photographed adequately with the standard lenses (especially zoom lenses) supplied with most compact and DSLR cameras. However, very few such lenses are able to capture some of the large optical effects visible in the sky (particularly the secondary bows of rainbows, the 46° halo, and other halo effects) and a specific wide-angle lens will be required. The angular size of these effects needs to be taken into account when purchasing wide-angle lenses. Manufacturers generally specify the angle covered by their particular lenses and this information helps to decide which lenses to use (be careful not to confuse the focal length of a lens – measured in mm – with the angle of coverage).

All-sky photographs taken with fish-eye lenses may be extremely striking, and such images are often taken to show auroral phenomena. However, these lenses are of limited use under most circumstances, because for maximum effect they need to be used from locations with a clear view of the sky with few obstructions on the horizon.

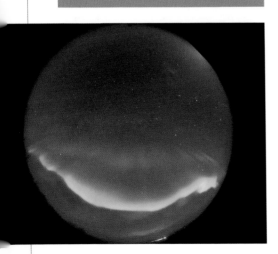

← All-sky image of the aurora, taken using a fish-eye lens. (P.-M. Hedén)

Angular sizes of certain optical effects

Effect	Radius	Overall size
Primary rainbow	42°	84°
46° halo	46°	92°
Secondary rainbow	51°	102°

The size of rainbows varies considerably, depending on the altitude of the Sun. In the extreme, when the Sun is on the horizon, a primary rainbow will form a perfect semi-circle and has a diameter of 84°, which is beyond the range of most standard lenses and even of the wide-angle setting of the majority of common zoom lenses. A secondary rainbow is far larger and will usually require a special wide-angle lens for all of it to be captured.

↑ Primary and secondary rainbows. *(Author)*

Panoramic images

Panoramic images are often particularly striking, and many cameras offer a setting to help in obtaining the individual images that can be later combined using image-manipulation software (often free), including those packages often offered by the camera's manufacturer. Generally the assistance offered consists of frame-lines visible in the viewfinder, helping to ensure that there is an adequate overlap between successive images. (Only the combination of several images can create true panoramas. The 'panoramic' functions that are offered on some cameras should be treated with caution as many of them merely crop top and bottom of a single image to produce a 'letter-box' effect that is not a true panorama.) Results from a succession of images taken to create a panorama normally work well, provided

that there is little rapid movement of the clouds. Ideally, a tripod should be used to ensure that the camera's viewpoint does not alter, but, with care, even hand-held photographs can be successfully combined using suitable software.

Note that because of the sometimes poorly defined features on cloud photographs, some software has difficulty in matching images. So, different types of software may provide wide variations in the final result, even when working with the same individual images. It pays to experiment with different software packages if possible.

Although it is rarely required for cloud photographs, it is also possible to join images vertically, not just side-by-side. In general this may involve just a couple of images, perhaps to show particularly striking deep clouds, or to illustrate mixed

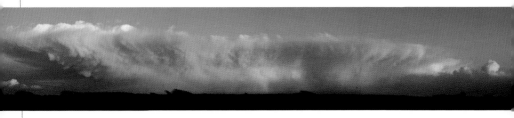

↑ A panoramic image of a cumulonimbus cluster. *(Author)*

skies with both low and high clouds. When images are joined horizontally, there is no real limit on the number of images that can be used, other than any limitations posed by the computer program that is being used. However, if several images are to be combined, attention should be given to the exposure settings. Generally, it is best to determine the exposure for the first image, and then lock this setting for subsequent photographs. When lighting conditions have changed over the sequence, it may be difficult or impossible to achieve successful matching, even with careful manipulation of individual images.

Exposure

The standard exposure settings on cameras assume an average subject, with a brightness range that can be averaged to a mid-grey tone. Because of this, sometimes clouds such as cumulus and cumulonimbus that are brilliantly illuminated by full sunlight fail to reproduce as brilliantly white, especially if the bright areas fill most of the frame. Snow scenes often suffer in the same way. Increasing the exposure manually (or switching to the snow/beach setting) will generally improve the detail captured. Most compact and DSLR cameras allow exposure compensation to make the final, overall image lighter or darker. This may be used to lighten the

brightest areas, but experimentation may be required to ensure that important highlight detail is not lost. Some cameras, including the most sophisticated smartphone cameras, provide a choice as to which part of an image should be used to set the exposure. Even here, however, it is generally assumed by the manufacturers that this small area should appear as a mid-grey tone, so increased exposure will still be necessary. Those cameras that allow highlight spot metering are the most successful in obtaining correct exposure for such difficult subjects.

Polarising filters

If it is assumed that a lens hood is used whenever necessary, the next most useful accessory for photographing clouds is a suitable polarising filter. Rotation of the filter will lighten or darken clouds or the sky background and may therefore reveal features that are otherwise difficult to see. A polarising filter, hand-held in front of the eye, is often useful in detecting details with purely visual observation. The degree of the effect obtained will vary, depending on the exact circumstances, particularly the location of the clouds with respect to the Sun. Polarisers have the greatest influence when clouds are about 90° from the Sun, and will have little effect when the Sun is directly behind the photographer, and none when clouds are silhouetted against the Sun. At 90° from the Sun, a polarizer may darken the sky considerably, sometimes making it appear almost black. This may detract from the aesthetic qualities of the photograph, so needs to be used with caution.

For photography, a circular, rather than linear, polariser should be used, to avoid introducing problems with any automatic exposure control, and with internal reflections in the camera, such as from the mirror in a DSLR. (The sheet plastic polarisers are normally of the linear type and are quite suitable for visual use, but not photographically.) A filter that screws onto the camera's lens is preferable, but this is not possible with some compact cameras. In this case, it is perfectly feasible to hold the polariser in front of the eye, turn it to obtain the desired result and, keeping the same orientation, hold the polariser in front of the lens whilst taking the photograph. Provided the polariser is large enough to cover the lens completely, even if held slightly off-centre, this method is perfectly feasible. With lightweight compact cameras it is usually possible to do this, hand-holding the camera, but use of a tripod will make it much easier. Although polarising filters absorb some light, in general the camera's exposure system will make the appropriate compensation.

The two photographs shown below demonstrate the significant difference that a polarising filter may make. The first photograph was taken with the filter rotated to accentuate details in the distant, white clouds. The filter was rotated by exactly 90° degrees before the second photograph was taken.

Stereo photography

An often-neglected form of photography is stereo photography. Although very popular in Victorian times, it has fallen out of fashion. However, at times it may be particularly valuable when studying clouds, in that it helps to distinguish one part of a cloud from another. In addition, it also helps to illustrate how clouds have a three-dimensional form – they are not just the basically flat objects that they appear to be in most photographs.

Taking stereo photographs is not difficult and may be carried out with any type of camera. There are various methods; indeed too many for them all to be described in detail here. Although dedicated stereo photographers may use two cameras, it is perfectly feasible to take one photograph of a particular cloud, move sideways, and take another photograph. Nowadays, there is computer software (including free packages) that use the two

🡐 🡓 The same clouds photographed with two orientations of a polarising filter. *(Author)*

↑ A stereo pair of clouds over the Hunter Valley in New South Wales. *(Duncan Waldron)*

individual photographs to produce either a stereo pair, or a single, two-colour image (known as an anaglyph), which is then viewed with suitable coloured glasses.

Stereo pairs of images may be viewed in two different ways. The simplest (and in many ways the best), is the 'crossed-eyes' method. In this, the two images are printed or viewed side-by-side, but the eyes are crossed until the two images fuse into a single, three-dimensional image. The image shown here may be viewed in this way. The two dots printed beneath the individual images help in fusing the two images. Bring the two dots together, and the main image will appear correctly.

This 'crossed-eyes' method has the big advantage that it may be used with any format of image. Unfortunately, some people are completely unable to cross their

↓ An anaglyph stereo image of clouds over the Hunter Valley in New South Wales. *(Duncan Waldron)*

eyes and view images in this way. They then need to use a special stereoscopic viewer, that uses two separate printed images, and has a lens in front of each eye to achieve the final stereo fusion. Again unfortunately, this method is really only suitable for portrait-format images (or square ones), and not for the landscape-format found with most cloud photographs.

The anaglyph, or two-colour method, has some advantages for anyone who is unable to use the 'crossed-eyes' technique, but again it can prove difficult to certain people, who find it difficult to fuse the two images, especially if there is a large amount of detail (and thus many separate colour edges) in the photograph.

Finally, it should be noted that most modern cameras of all types offer video facilities. Although these are unlikely to be required for the majority of cloud photographs, videos of fast-changing events such as waterspouts and other whirls will be of interest. Dedicated photographers have also produced some fascinating videos showing the changes in clouds and cloud cover over a period – sometimes as long as a whole day – using time-lapse imagery, taking one photograph every five or ten minutes.

→ The remnants of the Tower of the WInds, visible in Athens today. Two of the carved representations of the eight named winds are clearly visible in the frieze. *(Wikipedia Commons)*

Glossary

adiabatic
Without the addition or loss of heat.
Parcels of air in the atmosphere generally
rise and fall without the exchange of heat
with their surroundings.

anticyclone
A high-pressure region that is a source of
air that has subsided from higher altitudes,
and from which air flows out over the
surrounding area. The circulation around
an anticyclone is clockwise in the northern
hemisphere.

anticyclonic
Moving or curving in the same direction as
air circulating around an anticyclone, i.e.,
clockwise in the northern hemisphere,
anticlockwise in the southern.

convection
Transfer of heat by the motion of parcels of
a fluid such as air or water. In the
atmosphere this motion is predominantly
vertical. There are two forms of
convection: 'natural convection' in which
parcels or 'bubbles' of air are free to move
vertically driven by buoyancy effects; and
'forced convection' in which air is mixed
mechanically by eddies.

cyclone
A system in which air circulates around a
low-pressure core, with two distinct
meanings: 1) a 'tropical cyclone', a self-
sustaining tropical storm, also known as a
hurricane or typhoon; 2) an 'extratropical
cyclone' or depression, a low-pressure
area, which is one of the principal weather
systems in temperate regions.

cyclonic
Moving or curving in the same direction as
air that flows around a cyclone, i.e.,

anticlockwise in the northern hemisphere,
clockwise in the southern.

depression
The most frequently used term for a low-
pressure area. Air flows into a depresssion
and rises in its centre. Known technically
as an 'extratropical cyclone'. The wind
circulation around a depression is cyclonic
(anticlockwise in the northern hemisphere).

dewpoint
The temperature at which a particular
parcel of air, with a specific humidity, will
reach saturation. At the dewpoint, water
vapour will begin to condense into
droplets, giving rise to a cloud, mist or fog,
or depositing dew on the ground.

hurricane
One of several names for a potentially
destructive tropical cyclone, used in the
North Atlantic and eastern Pacific.

instability
The condition under which a parcel of air,
if displaced upwards or downwards, tends
to continue (or even accelerate) its motion.
The opposite is stability.

inversion
An atmospheric layer in which temperature
remains constant or increases with height.

jet stream
A narrow band of high-speed winds that lies
close to a breaks in the level of the
tropopause, with two main jet streams (the
polar-front and sub-tropical jet streams) in
each hemisphere. Other jet streams exist in
the tropics and at higher altitudes.

lapse rate
The rate at which temperature changes
with increasing height. By convention, the
lapse rate is positive when the

temperature decreases, and negative when it increases with height.

latent heat
The heat that is released when water vapour condenses into droplets or freezes into ice crystals. It is the heat that was originally required for the process of evaporation or melting.

mock sun
A halo effect, consisting of a bright point of light, often slightly coloured and with a white tail. It lies at the same altitude as the Sun and approximately 22° away from it. Known technically as a parhelion.

mesosphere
The atmospheric layer above the stratosphere, in which temperature decreases with height, reaching the atmospheric minimum at the mesopause, at an altitude of either 86 or 100km (depending on season and latitude).

occluded front
A front in a depression system, where the warm air has been lifted away from the surface, having been undercut by cold air. The front may, however, remain a significant source of cloud and precipitation.

parhelion
The technical term for a mock sun.

precipitation
The technical term for water in any liquid or solid form that is deposited from the atmosphere, and which falls to the ground. It excludes cloud droplets, mist, fog, dew, frost and rime, as well as virga.

stability
The condition under which a parcel of air, if displaced upwards or downwards, tends to return to its original position rather than continuing its motion.

stratosphere
The second major atmospheric layer from the ground, in which temperature initially remain constant, but then increases with height. It lies between the troposphere and the mesosphere, with lower and upper boundaries of approximately 8–20km (depending on latitude) and 50km, respectively.

supercooling
The conditions under which water may exist in a liquid state, despite being at a temperature below its nominal freezing point, 0°C. This occurs frequently in the atmosphere, often in the absence of suitable freezing nuclei. Supercooled water freezes spontaneously at a temperature of about -40°C [-40°F].

thermal
A rising bubble of air that has broken away from the heated surface of the ground. A thermal normally rises until it reaches the condensation level, where its water vapour condenses into droplets, giving rise to a cloud.

tropopause
The inversion that separates the troposphere from the overlying stratosphere. Its altitude varies from approximately 8 km at the poles to 18–20km over the equator.

troposphere
The lowest region of the atmosphere in which most of the weather and clouds occur. Within it, there is an overall decline in temperature with height.

virga
Trails of precipitation (as ice crystals or raindrops) from clouds that do not reach the ground, melting and evaporating in the drier air between the cloud and the surface.

wind shear
A change in wind direction or strength with a change of position. Vertical wind shear is when the wind strength increases with increasing height. Horizontal wind shear occurs if the wind strength changes with its position at a particular level.

Further reading

Identification, general and photographic studies

Chaboud, René. *How Weather Works* (Thames & Hudson, 1996).
Dunlop, Storm. *Collins Gem: Weather* (HarperCollins, 1999).
— *Collins Nature Guide: Weather* (HarperCollins, 2004).
— *Dictionary of Weather* (2nd edition, Oxford University Press, 2008).
— *Guide to Weather Forecasting* (revised printing, Philip's, 2013).
— *How to Identify Weather* (HarperCollins, 2002).
— *-How to Read the Weather* (National Trust, 2018)
— *Weather* (Cassell Illustrated, 2006/2007).
Eden, Philip. *Weatherwise* (Macmillan, 1995).
File, Dick. *Weather Facts* (Oxford University Press, 1996).
Hamblyn, Richard, and Meteorological Office. *The Cloud Book: How to Understand the Skies* (David & Charles, 2009).
— *Extraordinary Clouds* (David & Charles, 2009).
— *The Invention of Clouds* (Picador, 2001)
Ludlum, David. *Collins Wildlife Trust Guide: Weather* (HarperCollins, 2001).
Watts, Alan. *Instant Weather Forecasting* (Adlard Coles Nautical, 2000).
— *Instant Wind Forecasting* (Adlard Coles Nautical, 2001).
Whitaker, Richard (editor). *Weather: The Ultimate Guide to the Elements* (HarperCollins, 1996).
Williams, Jack. *The AMS Weather Book: The Ultimate Guide to America's Weather* (University of Chicago Press, 2009).

Journals

Weather, Royal Meteorological Society, Reading, UK (monthly).
Weatherwise, Heldref Publications, Washington DC, USA (bimonthly).

Internet links
CURRENT WEATHER

AccuWeather: www.accuweather.com.
   UK: www.accuweather.com/ukie/index.asp.
Australian Weather News: www.australianweathernews.com.
   UK station plots: www.australianweathernews.com/sitepages/charts/611_United_Kingdom.shtml.
BBC Weather: www.bbc.co.uk/weather.
CNN Weather: www.cnn.com/WEATHER/index.html.
Intellicast: http://intellicast.com.
ITV Weather: www.itv-weather.co.uk.
Unisys Weather: http://weather.unisys.com.

UK Meteorological Office: www.metoffice.gov.uk.
Forecasts: www.metoffice.gov.uk/weather/uk/uk_forecast_weather.html.
Hourly Weather Data: www.metoffice.gov.uk/education/teachers/latest-weather-data-uk.
Latest station plot: www.metoffice.gov.uk/data/education/chart_latest.gif.
Surface pressure charts: www.metoffice.gov.uk/public/weather/surface-pressure.
Explanation of symbols on pressure charts: www.metoffice.gov.uk/guide/weather/sysmbols#pressure-symbols.
Synoptic & climate stations (interactive map): www.metoffice.gov.uk/public/weather/climate-network/#?tab=climateNetwork.
Weather on the Web: http://wow.metoffice.gov.uk.
The Weather Channel: www.weather.com/twc/homepage.twc.
Weather Underground: www.wunderground.com.
Wetterzentrale: www.wetterzentrale.de/pics/Rgbsyn.gif.
Wetter3 (German site with global information): www.wetter3.de.
UK Met. Office chart archive: www.wetter3.de/Archiv/archiv_ukmet.html.

METEOROLOGICAL OFFICES, AGENCIES AND ORGANISATIONS
Environment Canada: www.msc-smc.ec.gc.ca.
European Centre for Medium-Range Weather Forecasting (ECMWF): www.ecmwf.int.
European Meteorological Satellite Organisation: www.eumetsat.int/website/home/index.html.
Intergovernmental Panel on Climate Change: www.ipcc.ch.
National Oceanic and Atmospheric Administration (NOAA): www.noaa.gov.
National Weather Service (NWS): www.nws.noaa.gov.
UK Meteorological Office: www.metoffice.gov.uk.
World Meteorological Organisation: www.wmo.int/pages/index_en.html.

SATELLITE IMAGES
Eumetsat: www.eumetsat.de.
Image library: www.eumetsat.int/website/home/Images/ImageLibrary/index.html.
Group for Earth Observation (GEO): www.geo-web.org.uk.
University of Dundee: www.sat.dundee.ac.uk.

SOCIETIES
American Meteorological Society: www.ametsoc.org/AMS.
Australian Meteorological and Oceanographic Society: www.amos.org.au.
Canadian Meteorological and Oceanographic Society: www.cmos.ca.
Climatological Observers Link (COL): https://colweather.ssl-01.com.
European Meteorological Society: www.wmwtsoc.org.
Irish Meteorological Society: www.irishmetsociety.org.
National Weather Association, USA: www.nwas.org.
New Zealand Meteorological Society: www.metsoc.org.nz.
Royal Meteorological Society: www.rmets.org.
TORRO: Tornado and Storm Research Organisation: http://torro.org.uk.

Index